A Blade of Grass

A Journey Transcending Grief and Loss
A Story of Hope

H. R. Maly

BALBOA
PRESS
A DIVISION OF HAY HOUSE

Balboa Press books may be ordered through booksellers or by contacting:

Balboa Press
A Division of Hay House
1663 Liberty Drive
Bloomington, IN 47403
www.balboapress.com
1-(877) 407-4847

ISBN: 978-1-4525-7597-1 (sc)
ISBN: 978-1-4525-7599-5 (hc)
ISBN: 978-1-4525-7598-8 (e)

Library of Congress Control Number: 2013910402

Printed in the United States of America.

Balboa Press rev. date: 06/25/2013

This book is dedicated to the memory of Daniel Joseph Maly,
and in honor of his mother, Grace Nicholson-Maly,
his three brothers, Timothy, Matthew, Michael,
his sister Megan, and my dear wife Maggie.

Contents

Introduction

This book took a number of years to write. I tried several times to complete it, but early on, my emotions prevailed and I simply set aside any notes I had managed to pen, with the thought that someday I would be able to write with a clear mind; I would be able to collect my thoughts and finish what I had set out to accomplish. I subscribe to the idea that "time heals all wounds." At last, I have completed my story.

My wish for you, since you are reading this book, is that you will benefit from this real-life story of how a father battled back from the devastation of losing a son, to finding not only peace, but a new view of life.

My hope is that you may receive insight and gain a sense of personal healing and happiness similar to that which I received, and for which I am forever grateful.

Many friends were there from the earliest days of my journey, and my heartfelt appreciation goes out to each and every one who offered support, words of wisdom, encouragement, and, most of all, their kindness and love. Thank you to Bud and Becky Baechler, Grace Nicholson-Maly, Bill Manning, Burnell and Trish Manley, Judith Marie Beck, Virginia Barta, John O'Connor, Andy Blomsness, Don Walz Jr., Dan Rukavina, Gil Hoel, Father John Supprenaut, Brother Raymond Long, Curt Holmquist, Dr. Ken and Gloria Wapnick, Alease Young, Judith Struck, Steve Loveland, and Phil Schmacher. And for her unwavering support, my wife, Maggie Cabral-Maly.

To all, thank you.

Part One
The Journey

Chapter One

A Thousand Miles

Nothing real can be threatened. Nothing unreal exists.
Herein lies the peace of God.
From *A Course in Miracles*, Volume 1

I was sleeping on the floor of Dan's bedroom, on a blow-up mattress. Tim, my oldest son, entered the room around one thirty in the morning, having just come home from his pizza delivery job. He shook me awake.

I jumped up in a fright, dazed and bleary-eyed. I checked Dan's pulse and screamed inside to myself, *Oh my God, he's gone!*

The realization that he had in fact made his transition into the spirit world hit me like a punch to my head. His long, courageous battle with cancer was over. I asked Tim to wake up his mother and the other boys, Matt and Mike, to let them know what happened.

We gathered in Dan's room and sat there, dumbfounded, as the reality of Dan's passing slowly began to sink in. Tears—many tears—flowed. We quietly prayed for him.

We didn't realize it at the time, but our family was being called to learn things about ourselves and each other that would change us permanently. The experience would take us on a journey of exploration, one we hadn't bargained for by any stretch of the imagination. Over the ensuing years, we would of course ask the probing questions about life and the vicissitudes that so many people like us experience.

As the days unfolded, I recalled that somewhere in the past I'd read sayings from a Chinese philosopher named Lao Tzu. One of his more famous sayings stated: "The journey of a thousand miles begins with one step." That evening was my first step in what would become an incredible journey. For me personally, it was, as they say, a *real game changer.*

*   *   *

The journey actually began when our family was young and we lived in Minnesota. Regardless of how beautiful the state is, life in Minnesota is a challenge, especially during the winter months of December through March.

I recall an especially mild winter when the warmth of the spring season seemed on its way earlier than usual.

My son Daniel, the second oldest of our four sons, had finished his daily newspaper delivery route to some sixty families in our neighborhood. Every morning, he would rise and shine at six o'clock and start his morning trek on his new ten-speed bicycle.

One morning, with the sun just peeking over the bluffs of the Mississippi River Valley, he entered the house. He sighed and said he was glad he was done delivering the papers and could get ready for school.

"Were there any problems with your paper delivery this morning, besides the chill in the air"? I asked.

As he rumbled into his room he said, "No, nothing to report. The only thing," he said in passing, "is this nagging tingling feeling I have in the fingers on my left hand."

Neither one of us paid much attention to that complaint, as mild as it was, since he always carried his newspaper bag with the strap over his left shoulder. We both thought the bag probably caused some strain on his arm which had radiated down to his fingers. So, as the days went on, he seemed pretty happy with the morning chore of delivering his newspapers.

Several days later, in the evening, he mentioned that his fingers were still tingling. His mom and I decided that he ought to go to St. Francis Medical Center in Lacrosse, Wisconsin, to have it checked out. X-rays were taken but nothing showed up that seemed out of place, so he began a physical therapy regimen.

Another week went by and still no change as the tingling sensation continued. Then a nurse friend suggested that we stop waiting and take Dan to the Mayo Clinic, which was an hour's drive west from the town where we lived. That was the beginning of a series of events that changed everything—or at least changed life as I knew it.

This is a story of miracles. Not only one or two, but many of them. As you read through the events that unfold in this journey, several miracles may be clear as they emerge. Others may not be as clear.

Throughout my writing, I refer to *A Course in Miracles*. By way of explanation, I offer a passage from the introduction to that book, contained in Volume 1 Text.

> This is a course in miracles. It is a required course. Only the time you take it is voluntary. Free will does not mean that you can establish the curriculum. It means only that you can elect what you want to take at a given time. The course does not aim at the teaching of love, for that is beyond what can be taught. It does aim, however, at removing the blocks to the awareness of love's presence, which is your natural inheritance. The opposite of love is fear, but what is all-encompassing can have no opposite. This course can be summed up very simply in this way:
>
> Nothing real can be threatened.
> Nothing unreal exists.
> Herein lies the peace of God.

Chapter one of volume I, *A Course in Miracles,* reads: "Miracles are both beginnings and endings, and so they alter the temporal order. They are always affirmations of re-birth, which seem to go back but really go forward. They undo the past in the present and release the future."

By extension of the impact his life had and has on me, this is also, in part, the story of Daniel Joseph Maly, a fifteen-year-old boy who, for two and a half years, fought gallantly to beat a cancer that eventually took him from this world. He didn't win the battle, but his legacy and ensuing "victory" have engendered a life spirit of love, hope, and forgiveness in those who knew him personally and in those who have come to learn of the healing power of who he was and how he lived his life.

But this is mostly the story of a father who is a beneficiary of Dan's life's purpose. I learned a great deal from his time with us, some of it very painful and yet some of it incredibly enlightening.

This is an exploration of how, as his dad, I learned to experience his "passing over" into the spirit world in a positive light. That required a transformation from an incredibly negative thought process steeped with bitterness and anger at the loss of my son, to a positive view of acceptance. However, this was more than the acceptance of the death of my child. The journey involved years of personal inner work to correct how I viewed the world and how I functioned in it.

Life situations occurred and brought great sadness when I was called to walk through the fire that brought purification. With much assistance from many people, change did eventually manifest itself in my life, and this book hopefully will shed light on how I interpreted initial events and tried to survive them. As I replaced old thought patterns, thus changing how I felt and reacted to those feelings, my life was ultimately transformed.

I share my reflections on the series of events that led to how I finally reinvented myself. The result is that I more than survived a traumatic experience; I grew stronger in my beliefs, became more spiritual, and now live with a deep and abiding faith in my Higher Power and my God. And what I hope for you, the reader, is that my reflections help you to see what's possible for yourself if you, too, are on a life-changing journey.

*   *   *

We finally made the decision to go to the Mayo Clinic, so we jumped in the car and headed for Rochester, Minnesota, convinced we'd wasted several precious days by not acting sooner.

Dan was taken into the emergency room immediately, and the physicians began to do all the necessary preliminary work to determine a diagnosis. They did a procedure called a myelogram (it's where they shoot a dye in the base of your spine and tip the patient upside down so the dye will flow along the spinal cord). That took all day and finally a series of tests revealed that he had a tumor or a mass located somewhere in the upper part of his neck.

Not good news.

Without much delay, the surgeons decided to perform a laminectomy. This is a surgical procedure to remove the lamina—the back part of the vertebra that covers your spinal canal. Also known as decompression surgery, laminectomy is generally used only when more conservative treatments, such as medication and physical therapy, have failed to relieve symptoms. It also may be recommended if symptoms are severe or worsening dramatically.

The surgery took a little over six hours. We waited and waited for word from someone on the medical staff. The day dragged on. As we waited, some dear friends of ours, Bud and Becky Baechler, stayed with us during those long, worrisome hours. (In fact, they stayed with us even through Dan's postoperative forty-eight hours.)

I paced back and forth in the waiting room. I will never forget the fear of not seeing my son alive again, of not being able to say good-bye, continually wondering why the surgery was taking so long. It was suffocating.

Then I was bombarded with thoughts of why hadn't I taken action sooner. Was I so wrapped up in my work and daily routine that I'd missed taking care of a potential problem? Shouldn't I have known that it could have been a problem? *Guilt.* I struggled with good old-fashioned parental guilt. I was stuck. I felt like a fool and, worse yet, I believed I had failed one of my children.

When pacing provided no relief, I tried to sit and read a magazine, the articles of which made absolutely no sense. Everything in life suddenly seemed totally meaningless. Who cared who was bombing which country or who was stealing whatever from someone? All of that was now completely irrelevant in light of the fact that something was stealing the life of my perfectly healthy son.

I needed a smoke. Hadn't smoked in thirty years, but I needed a smoke. I felt like I was in a box and couldn't get out—trapped. *Where the hell could I go?*

No, wait, maybe *this* was hell! How far away was the nearest bar? I wanted to do something, to be somewhere else. I didn't want to be in a sanitary hospital waiting room. The whole damn thing was way too scary and painful. My mind ran wild with uncontrollable thoughts of failure.

Heck, I was a trained professional athlete. I was trained to win, not to fail. I could hear my old coach preaching, "Failure is not an option, winning is the only thing." As I sat there, I thought, *What kind of bullshit is that? Let's put some of those guys in this situation and then tell me about what it feels like to fail.* Obviously my anger had begun to cloud my judgment.

Bud and Becky rescued me, albeit for a short time, when they came over and saw immediately that the pressure of waiting and wondering was taking a toll on me. They encouraged me to go for a walk with them, so we toured the coffee shop. Doesn't sound like much, but for all I knew at the time, it could have been Disney World.

Bud and Becky were living examples of what true friends are all about. Bud's brother, Bill, and his wife, Sally, took over for them and watched Bud and Becky's four small daughters so they could stay and visit with us. It is a friendship that I will always cherish. What they did for us is something that, even to this day, I find remarkable.

Dan was wheeled into surgery around ten o'clock in the morning. The day slowly edged toward late afternoon and as the sun started to set, I grew incredibly concerned for Dan's survival. I knew he was a strong kid. He'd recently been named Most Valuable Swimmer on the Winona, Minnesota, junior high swim team, and he was involved in baseball and football as well. He was in great physical shape. Still, the length of time he was in surgery terrified me.

After what seemed an eternity, a nurse came out to talk to us and reported that we could see Dan in the recovery room, but the surgeon wanted to have a word with us first.

The doctor told us they'd almost lost Dan because the tumor had grown around his spinal cord at the location of the seventh cervical vertebra, the one that controlled breathing.

After the first surgery was completed, Dan wasn't breathing on his own so they had to open him up again to see what had caused the problem. They couldn't find anything wrong. When they finished the second time, he began to breathe on his own. So that's what the delay had been all about.

They thought the entire tumor had been removed. But, to be sure, radiation and chemotherapy would be part of his post-op treatment regimen. What they didn't tell us at the time was that young people who had that type of cancer didn't have a very good survival rate!

After the meeting with the surgeon, we went into the recovery room and saw that Dan was all wired up. It seemed like he had tubes everywhere. He certainly couldn't talk with the tube apparatus down his throat, so I came close to the bed and spoke to him. I told him how proud I was of his strength and courage.

He blinked his eyes as though he was saying "Yes." Then his eyes seemed to be pleading, as though he wanted to speak with us. We devised a system that would allow him to spell out words by a blink or two of his eyes.

He spelled out B-U-M-M-E-R, and I acknowledged that he was right, it was a bummer for him to be so sick.

When I left the room to get some air, completely brokenhearted and feeling totally helpless, my determination to do everything to save him was intense.

Thankful that Dan's mom, Grace, and Bud and Becky had stayed with him in the recovery room, I headed for the elevator to buy some coffee for everyone from the cafeteria downstairs.

As I stepped to the elevator to press the down button, all my emotions hit like a freight train, and I began to cry uncontrollably. Embarrassed, I tried to pull myself together, when an elderly gentleman touched my arm.

"Son, it's okay to shed those tears. Somehow, and I don't have an answer for you, but I know that someday all of this will make sense to you. Have hope. It will, in time, be okay."

Over the years I have come to appreciate that teachers arrive in our lives to give us lessons we need to learn. Some of those lessons come from individuals we like and feel are kind souls and we appreciate what they have to say. At other times, individuals come into our lives we judge as unkind and don't have a particular liking toward them. The lessons, however, are there for us to see and understand, no matter the "package" that they come in.

I've never forgotten his words. Truth be told, he was correct. The irony is, however, that it took many years and considerable personal work on my part to change my beliefs, which eventually led to a positive change in my life.

I also find it curious how an incident such as this one came into my life to make other experiences meaningful. I've thought back to that elevator scene on numerous occasions, especially at moments when I'm comforting a friend in a difficult situation. That gentleman allowed me to be who I was at that point in time and gave me permission to express my feelings. I was allowed to be in the moment. I was allowed to be human.

Many times since that day, I have offered the very same words to others who have been in difficult situations. Because I've learned those words to be true, I'm comfortable sharing them with others at times when no other words can help.

Reflection: During all the years since that experience, I realize now that it did wonders for me to understand that it takes a real man to cry when life hurts. Getting in touch with one's feelings is really where it's at, in my estimation.

*   *   *

I returned to the recovery room to see that Dan was resting comfortably. A nurse came in and asked us to accompany her to Pathology to talk to the doctor about Dan's condition.

God bless all the nurses who assist families during times of stress and confusion. Our nurse's name was Ingrid, and she had a sense of peace about her which was very comforting. As we rode in the elevator, all was quiet. Glancing over at Ingrid, I noticed her eyes filling with tears. I knew then that the meeting with the pathologist was going to be difficult.

I was right. We sat down for our consultation, and the doctor told us bluntly that Dan's tumor was cancerous. My head shot back as though someone had hit me in the middle of my forehead with a mallet. Dan had *cancer.* The information didn't take hold at first. Shock took over and I felt dazed from the news. I was lightheaded and a little sick to my stomach. Our conversation ended, and we headed in silence for the door. Ingrid said she was so, so very sorry.

We thanked her for her care and concern, and made our way back to Dan's room. I stood there looking at him in shock and wondered what all of this meant.

Where did we go from here? Would I be strong enough as a parent, to survive this? The answer came flooding into my heart and my mind—yes, yes, and yes, I would survive. I remembered my Catholic upbringing and pledged to myself that I would do everything in my power to see that a miracle would indeed save Dan.

Because of the severity of the operation, Dan was kept in the intensive care unit for forty-eight hours to make sure he continued to breathe on his own.

At the end of the day, we decided to stay at a motel near the hospital instead of going to the Ronald McDonald House. Despite the offer of understanding and solace available there, my wife and I needed time alone and just didn't want to talk to anyone.

In hindsight, that decision wasn't the smartest we ever made. As that first night rolled onward, the world became smaller and smaller and it seemed as though the walls of the room were closing in on me. I thought back over my life wondering if ever there was a time I'd felt so much confusion, doubt, and flat-out fear. I couldn't remember any time like it. Sleep didn't come to me that night. Fear of the unknown threatened to choke us both.

The next several days were a blur. Our dear friends stayed close by, and Bud's brother, Bill, even came by for a visit, which was great because it meant that someone else from our small community was also nearby and concerned about us.

Even so, I can remember feeling trapped as I sat there in the waiting room. What the hell was I going to do and how would I be able to handle the challenges? So much self-doubt and guilt flooded my thoughts. I actually began to calculate that with my credit card I could grab a cab to the airport, be on a plane to New Zealand, and escape everything before anyone would know where I was.

Of course, the reality is that we have to play with the cards dealt to us. We may not want to walk through the fire, but that's what we are called to do.

After several weeks in the hospital, Dan was ready to be released. We took him home to begin the recovery from his ordeal.

It was difficult to see him that way. His once-strong athletic body now moved with hesitation, somewhat wobbly at times. The laminectomy surgery left him with a posture that was ramrod straight. He actually looked as though he was half the size of his former self.

Though all four of my sons were gifted athletically, Dan and my son Matthew were probably the fastest runners in our family. All of the boys seemed to really enjoy being involved in athletic programs and it had always been a great pleasure for me to assist my sons in each of the sports they chose to participate in. In light of Dan's delight of sports, his situation seemed particularly unfair.

Memory flashback: One day I sat in the bleachers watching a junior high school football game. Dan was one of the running backs on his team. When he carried the ball and hit the line, he busted through, and with a burst of speed and quickness he raced down the field. The other kids didn't have a chance to catch him; he was gone and headed for the end zone before they knew what happened. I heard several of the other fathers say: "Wow, who is that kid?" "He runs like a deer." "No one is going to catch him!" I wanted to jump up and shout, "Hey, that's my son!" As football ended, Dan switched to his first love, swimming. Although his swim team practices were long and strenuous, he was coming into his own as a breaststroke swimmer. He was developing strong upper-body strength by virtue of all the exercises he was put through. He was strong, agile and, in a silent way, oh so competitive.

Reflection: It's a gift to have the opportunity to see your child excel, be it in a sport or in the theater, academically or whatever activity they love being involved in. It's all about their growth and happiness. I didn't always understand that.

Chapter Two

Dads

"All humans exist within the absolute Oneness of God.
We cannot escape who we are or opt out of our soul's journey to God.
In other words, there is no such thing as being outside of, or disconnected
from, the Oneness. There is only the state of becoming aware
of your existence within the Whole."
—Linda Howe, from the book, *How to Read the Akashic Records*

Several days before we drove home from the Mayo Clinic, Dan and I sat on a bench outside Saint Marys Hospital in downtown Rochester, Minnesota. We talked about how he felt, how his body had changed, and what he wanted do in the months ahead.

He said, "You know, Dad, I think the thing that I'm really disappointed about is that my body has changed so much and I feel so puny and look so skinny." He sat quietly for several minutes and then he continued. "To tell you the truth, I'm not sure what my ultimate goal is now. But I want to get back to the way I was physically, before all this happened to me. I guess if I work at it, it'll happen."

"So what do think you need to do, and how do you think you could make that happen?" I asked. "What timeline do you think you ought to come up with?"

He said, "Well, basically I don't have any set time frame. I haven't thought about that yet. I guess I'll work at it for as long as it takes."

So, as we sat there, we came up with a plan which included me becoming his trainer-in-residence, helping him to regain his strength and his health. Perhaps we couldn't get back to where he once was, but we thought we could get pretty close to it. My desire to help Dan in his recovery became my focus, and I was ready for the challenge.

Memory flashback: My background growing up in Astoria, in the Borough of Queens, New York City, as well as my athletic experiences and competitive instincts, played a major role in how I dedicated my time to helping Dan. In the household I grew up in, several common themes were heard. "We don't have much money, but we have a lot of fun," was one, and, "You know, we are shanty Irish, after all; we're supposed to be poor." It isn't surprising that I grew up thinking that all Irish, no matter who they were, were poor. *Thank God,* I used to think, *that my heritage was also half Czech.*

My neighborhood was a melting pot of immigrant families mostly from Greece and Italy, as well as the European and Irish contingents. The men and women in those families were hardworking and lived by a strict code of ethics and values not to be questioned—by anybody. The blue-collar class was who we were and we were damn proud of it. Most of the men in our family either became cops in the NYPD or firemen in the NYFD. No one was urged to go to college; it wasn't in our parents' nature to encourage an extended education for their children.

My dad was an ironworker in NYC all his adult life and worked hard to give us a very good family life. I don't ever remember wanting for anything. But, then again, I didn't need much since I was wrapped up in playing baseball and basketball most of the time. I basically lived and grew up on the street, honing my athletic skills playing stickball or in the schoolyard playing strike-box.

It stood to reason that when I became of age, and according to our family values, I would either be a cop or a fireman. I had other plans, however, as I had had an exceptionally successful athletic career in high school. Suddenly the world offered another opportunity for me to look at, college and possibly a pro career in baseball. And so I made my choice. I was hooked, like so many young guys my age. The dream to make it to the major leagues as a professional baseball player became my dream and my goal. My competitiveness was at an all-time high.

Senior year in high school brought another exceptional year involving athletics. In baseball I pitched a no-hitter and several one-hitters. My basketball success yielded several college scholarships from small schools in the East. But, true to my dream, I signed a contract to play for the Cincinnati Redlegs as a pitcher. I was on my way.

As I matured in later years, I always encouraged my sons to dream big. To think about what they wanted in life and go for it. I said to them many times (probably more than they needed to hear), "You can't experience the reality of what you want unless you dream the dream." And so it came to pass. Tim, our oldest son, became an excellent swimmer and runner, and Matthew and Michael both excelled at playing basketball.

Reflection: There is no escaping where we come from or what our background is and who our parents are. No matter what our heritage is, it is the foundation of our lives. It seems as though we either embrace it or try to figure out how to get beyond it. In reality, I believe it is what it is.

The determination to succeed that I had acquired as an athlete carried over to my plan to help Dan gain back his strength and become healthy again. I desperately wanted our family to get back into some type of a normal routine as well. It wasn't all that easy for us because we were constantly aware of Dan's health challenges, constantly thinking positive thoughts, to help him get well. We'd gone through so much as a family that we couldn't just put it behind us. Trying to be upbeat with a firm determination to help Dan challenged all of us.

* * *

The rehabilitation plan to bring Dan back to his pre-cancer state of physical fitness included my meeting him during his school days at the junior high school.

The YMCA was located only two blocks away from his school, and he had prearranged to have his physical education classes switched to the "Y" where we would work together in his rehab program. He did very well for the fourteen months he remained in remission.

Those were days when our family had a semblance of normality. Our other three sons, Timothy, Matthew, and Michael, each had their own activities at school to keep them busy. The day-to-day routine that most families have with active children returned to our household.

I continued my work at Saint Mary's University, and Grace was active as the school nurse at Madison Middle School. Prior to Dan's initial diagnosis, however, we had an exchange student from Ireland who came to stay with us for two weeks.

Alan was a delightful boy, about the same age as Dan. Alan kept us laughing and entertained. He was a blessing to have in our home, with his lighthearted spirit, and his Irish accent was great fun to listen to. Alan especially loved McDonald's french fries. Having Alan as a part of our family was great for us and he helped ease the fear of everything we were experiencing.

During those months of remission Dan showed signs of being healthier and getting stronger physically. Even though he still had that ramrod-straight posture as a result of his surgery, he tried hard to look like a normal teenager again.

* * *

In the years before we experienced this trauma in our lives, I'd mentioned to each of my sons that since I was a former professional athlete, I could and would help them in any sport they wanted to pursue. In fact, I encouraged them to play either a team sport or a solo sport such as tennis.

I cautioned them, however, that I also wanted them to pursue playing a musical instrument. I felt that just being a jock wasn't enough. I believed they would thank me later on in their lives because they would be more rounded individuals and wouldn't have missed out on some very interesting experiences both musically and socially.

Tim swam and played the violin. Dan was a swimmer, played football, and took up the cornet. Matt played basketball and decided on the bass guitar. Michael played basketball and the alto sax.

Memory flashback: The blue-collar neighborhood I grew up in had its own unwritten code of how a kid should behave and what he could and could not do. It was a code that 99 percent of the kids lived by for no other reason than fear of retribution from the older kids. Namely, it was totally cool and acceptable to play stickball on Twenty-Fourth Street in Astoria or to play strike-box and hoops in the schoolyard at P.S. 122. Baseball, basketball, football, and soccer were also acceptable. And the only reason some kids played soccer was because many of the families were from Greece, Italy, or some European country.

What we didn't want to do was walk home from school with a violin case in our possession because that was *not* acceptable. Of course we could play the violin, but we would be subjected to verbal abuse and a label that wasn't nice. Who wanted to be labeled a "fruit" or a "sissy"? Oh, and we didn't play tennis either—they had a name for that as well. Consequently, being in an environment where people had such a myopic view of the world kept many young people from experiencing a rather important slice of life . . . the arts.

*   *   *

I think back to my own dad and how he was such a good parent for me. He was an excellent example and a great teacher regarding how to sacrifice personal time in order to help his children. I didn't catch on to that until years later, when I had commitments that involved my sons' activities. It's said that we tend to parent our children the way we were parented. I believe that to be true.

It wasn't until I had children of my own that I realized what my dad did for me. He was an ironworker in the trades in NYC and had the credentials of being a master welder, which I later came to understand was significant in his industry. He could weld anything: iron, steel, aluminum, you name it and his work was first class. He spent 8½ years working on the World Trade Center, and many evenings when he came home he would suggest that we hop in the car and drive to the local ball field in Astoria Park to play catch. Still in his work clothes, he would get behind home plate and "warm me up." He knew, of course, that I wanted a career in professional baseball as a pitcher, so he took it upon himself to help me fulfill that dream. As he crouched down behind home plate, I stood on the pitcher's mound and pitched to him. Even though he wasn't a skilled athlete, he did his best to catch the pitches I threw at his mitt.

He always encouraged me to give it my best shot, meaning to throw the ball as fast as I could. As I grew older I would always hold back. Heck, I was throwing the ball 92 to 95 mph and didn't want to hurt him. The irony is that we both became more skilled because of those practice sessions. He actually became a good catcher, perhaps not at Yogi Berra's level, but certainly good enough for me. Thinking back on those days, I realize what he actually did for me. He sacrificed his time and energy to help me. But more important was the bond that formed between father and son. I hope I passed along some of that to my sons as they were growing up.

I felt that bond profoundly the day I said good-bye to my dad. He was in a hospital bed in Albany, New York, having just come through surgery. I stood by his bedside and although he couldn't talk, we looked at each other, and I said, "Dad, do you know that I love you?"

A tear rolled down his cheek and he nodded his head yes. Unfortunately, that was the last time I saw him and yet that memory gives me great comfort to this day. Being able to say good-bye is a blessing.

Reflection: *Maturing to be the person we truly want to be is our God-given right. We have the free will do as we please; to be surrounded by those who protect and nurture us from infancy to adulthood. To allow that experience to happen is a marvelous gift in our lives.*

It was from this perspective that I wanted my sons to have the experience of being musicians or participating in school plays, to play in the school orchestra, or form a rock 'n' roll band if they wanted to.

The easy part was convincing them to participate. The challenge was getting everyone to their various practices and games, since we lived six miles out of town in the rural countryside of Minnesota. But our commitment to them paid off in all they each accomplished.

One day I heard a song by Dan Fogelberg, titled, "Longer Than," coming from Dan's room. It seemed that one part of the song, a solo played by a horn, was being repeated over and over again. I called down to his room to ask why he kept playing that part of the record.

He said, "Oh, I'm not playing the record, I'm playing that part of the song myself on my cornet."

I was totally amazed because I couldn't distinguish between the version he played on his horn and the version coming from the record, he'd become that good.

He continued to practice his horn and continued to work out at the YMCA. He got stronger as his level of energy increased.

He decided to join the school's marching band, and in early May he marched in the annual La Crescent, Minnesota, Apple Festival Parade. Dan's school was well represented, and as a marching band they sounded very good.

Like many of the parents, we went to the parade to support Dan and his classmates. He looked great that day and did well considering the long distance the kids had to march in that parade. It was bittersweet: I was really proud of him, and yet it was sad to see him all decked out in his school colors and neat uniform. He looked so frail and yet he held his head up high, true to who Dan was.

He managed a smile and a nod of his head as he strode on by us, unfazed by the fact that he was a little wobbly as he walked. I certainly learned a great deal about what true courage is just by being with Dan and watching him make his way through all of the trials and tribulations he faced.

Time and again, Dan showed us both his courage and his mettle. According to Webster, "courage" implies firmness of mind and will in the face of danger or extreme difficulty and "mettle" suggests an ingrained capacity for meeting strain or stress with fortitude and resilience. I would add that Dan also had a very real sense of style and grace, especially through his most difficult times.

However, preceding those days with the high school marching band, I'm reminded of when Dan was in the Mayo Clinic, after his surgery. I would drive up to visit him every day to see how he was doing, hoping he was feeling better. During the first couple of weeks after his initial surgery,

I noticed that he looked pale and was still pretty weak. He couldn't move his arms or legs, but gradually he began to show signs of mending.

I came into his room one afternoon and saw a group of physicians gathered around his bed and immediately thought the worse. Thankfully it was only one physician and a group of student interns examining him as a part of their teaching routine.

When they left the room, Dan said, "I'm okay, except for the fact that all these 'white coats' keep coming in here to tickle my feet to see if I'll jump." We both laughed.

Then he said, "Hey Dad, I want to show you something, because I think I'm getting better."

He had great determination written on his face, the same determination I'd seen when he was on the blocks at a swimming meet at school. He slowly began to lift his arm off the bed and up toward his head.

I was amazed he could do that since he still looked so fragile and weak. Joy rushed through me as I told him how amazed and proud I was.

He said, "Oh, just wait, I'm not done yet." He began to bring his arm back down. "Look, I can wiggle my toes as well."

My mind flashed back to that day when I was in the stands at the football game, so proud that he was such a good player. And now, seeing him battle back, my heart was bursting. The happiness and pride I felt for him was something that went way beyond anything I'd ever felt before. His courage to fight was awesome and inspiring.

Chapter Three

Courage, Mettle, and Grace

"Becoming whole does not mean being perfect, but being completed.
It does not necessarily mean happiness, but growth. It is often painful,
but, fortunately, it is never boring. It is not getting out of life what we
think we want, but is the purification and development of the soul."
—John A. Sanford, *Healing and Wholeness*

As I walk through life now, I realize that I have been blessed to have known a soul such as Dan. What I bring to situations, no matter how trivial or difficult they may seem, is fashioned in large part by what I learned from watching my son fight. He never wavered as he faced hurdle after hurdle, as he battled his cancer with courage, mettle, and grace.

Shortly after Dan's passing, a dear friend of mine, Bill, an attorney in a prestigious law firm in Minneapolis, asked that I assist him with a fundraising project which was in the initial planning stages.

It was to be called Camphill Minnesota, located near St. Cloud, MN. I was not familiar with Camphill, but soon learned that it is an anthroposophical organization born of the genius of the German philosopher Rudolf Steiner.

Bill, who is a very spiritually advanced soul, is also an anthroposophist, and he suggested that I first visit an established facility in Copake, NY. (For those who may not know what anthroposophy is, it's a philosophy based on the view that the human intellect has the ability to contact spiritual worlds and centers on human development. It was formulated in the early twentieth century and today the Swiss-based society has branches around the world.) I soon came to know all about Camphill as an initiative inspired by anthroposophy. There are 119 Camphill communities in twenty-one countries throughout Europe, North America, southern Africa, and Asia. They are residential "life-sharing" communities and schools for adults and children with learning disabilities, mental health problems, and other special needs, which provide services and support for work, learning, and daily living. (Wikipedia source)

The facility in Upstate New York is a working farm of about 350 acres. "Normal" families live with and care for physically and mentally challenged adults as though they were all part of the same family.

I believe there are approximately twenty to twenty-five homes there, wherein married couples with children also care for seven to eight mentally and/or physically challenged adults. My three-day visit was a game changer, as it brought me to a new level of awareness about people and about life.

On the first day, when I entered the home where I was to stay during my visit, I was apprehensive. I'd never been involved in a situation surrounded by so many challenged adults. It was flat-out scary.

*   *   *

My first experience was with a fellow named Robert, who had a severe tic syndrome. It manifested when he was in conversation with someone. His hands would fly up over his head or around his neck in jerking motions.

Robert was my host. I sat and talked with him in the foyer of his home as we awaited the dinner bell to ring, summoning us to the evening meal. We talked for about an hour and I was totally mystified as to how I would make it through the situation.

The next day I spent time with a fellow named Michael, who was completely noncommunicative. That evening after the dinner meal, I was invited to visit another home of a now-dear friend, Aase. Everyone in the home was involved in batiking, dying material with exquisitely designed artwork. Michael came up to me and stood close to my shoulder. He didn't do anything, but merely kept following me around the table where the members of his family were engaged in this project that I was invited to view. When I moved to the left, Michael moved to the left. When I went the other way, Michael went the other way. Although he was kind, peaceful, and seemed very friendly, I was nonplussed by it all.

Later that evening Aase asked me if I wondered what Michael was up to during my visit at her home. I told her yes and I wasn't sure what I should do. She explained it in simplistic terms.

"Hank," she said, "if you couldn't talk and yet you wanted to show a guest that he was welcome in your home, what would you do to show them you liked them and were glad they came to visit?" She explained further. "All Michael was trying to do was to welcome you into his home in the only way he knew to say that you're welcome here."

And there it was for me . . . another sign of courage, mettle, and grace.

On the flight back home I reflected on my experience with Robert. Guess what? During our conversation, he'd asked me a series of questions about where I lived, what kind of work I did, my marital status, my wife's name, and so on.

Aren't those the same types of questions that we "normal" people ask as we visit with a guest? And there you have it . . . another lesson in courage, mettle, and grace.

Reflection: Rudolf Steiner advocated that all human beings were born equally. His thought is that human existence on earth is not linear with the brightest on one end and the challenged on the other end of the spectrum. Rather, he believed that it is circular, where everyone is a child of God sharing his or her gifts as an equal for all to witness. He also advocated that individuals chose to be incarnate on this physical plane as a way of sharing the gifts that they have been given.

I have often been asked about what it is like to lose a son. My response unequivocally is this: I haven't lost a son; I have gained an insight into that which we perceive to be the real world, because I was privileged to have been a part of my son's life while he was here.

I realize now that I have been blessed because he came and showed us what true courage, mettle, and grace really are. Like Robert and Michael each showing me how we can pass along the beauty of who we are with the gifts that we have, even though we might be perceived as "different."

All that we see is not necessarily real. It's a matter of knowing how to let our light shine in this world. As I hope you will see later in this book, this life is real for us because we can experience it through our senses, which we use to reveal what it is to us. The spirit world is only real to us if we can learn how to be present to and open to it.

* * *

Family life in our home continued on a "normal" path, with everyone involved in many activities. The days continued to roll along as we enjoyed our time together.

The boys had two beautiful rust-colored golden retrievers. The three boys settled on taking care of the mother golden, Miss Megan, who initially was the newest member to our family. Dan cared for a pup and dubbed him Rusty Bones.

As the dogs grew in size and weight, it was rather comical at times to see the boys trying to ride the dogs as though they were little ponies. Dan and Rusty became inseparable. And so man's best friend became boy's best friend. Rusty grew to be a strong dog, and when Dan took him for a walk, a better description is probably to say that Rusty was taking Dan for a walk. Everything seemed to be going well for us.

We continued to attend Sunday Mass at our local church in Winona and participated in many of the social events as well. The best treat for the boys was staying after Mass to enjoy the donuts and juice. Fellowship time was a great incentive for everyone to behave and not goof around during Mass. Hey, sometimes you have to do what you have to do!

Dan was quickly approaching the age when it was appropriate for him to take religious instruction in preparation for confirmation into the Catholic faith. So he began his instructions and continued to attend junior high school. As the weeks went by, we all began to realize that Dan was looking tired and a little pale. He insisted he was doing fine and that he really wanted to be confirmed in the church.

I was reluctant to attend church every Sunday because I wanted the boys to understand that God was not tied to a building like a church, but that God did in fact reside in our hearts and if we looked inside we were sure to find Him. Sure, churches could be holy places, but God is no less present if we're sitting on top of a bluff on a sunny fall day enjoying His creation. My point was that I believed that God was everywhere and in all things, and if we looked within, sure enough, we could and would come to an understanding of our Creator.

Dan had a marvelous religious education teacher. We could tell from the way Dan talked about religion that he was growing closer and closer to a personal relationship with God through Jesus Christ. As an assignment he was asked to craft a statement of his beliefs. The following is what he wrote:

My Creed (what I believe about my best friend)

I believe that God is our past, our present, and our destiny. He is the Almighty being that has created us and given us the right to live as we wish. He loves every one of us no matter what other people say. Everyone in His book is equal, regardless of what is going on in the world.

I believe that everything in our lives has a purpose. God decides if the certain thing is good or bad because we weren't given the right to judge God's actions in our lives.

I believe that Jesus died for us to enable everyone to rise up into heaven if they choose to have a strong will and reject sin and follow God. He has given us the Bible for the same reason, to help guide us through our life. It is filled with teachings, guidelines, and answers. All these are there if you can find them. Because if you find your own meaning, your interpretation will be your own belief and not somebody else's belief.

I believe the Holy Spirit comes to you when you are ready to be brought fully into the church. I believe that when I receive the Holy Spirit my spirit will be fully initiated into God's world, and I will start a spiritual growth spurt.

I believe Christ promised eternal life because at the end God wants to be united with all the people who suffered or were tempted or had many troubles and barriers to climb over or just plain had problems, and still stayed close with God and believed.

I believe that I am like an instrument of God. He uses me in His own ways by directing my life the way He wants it.

And I believe that whatever happens to me or, rather, my body, if it's with pain or without, it's all for God.

Chapter Four

Metastasis

"I want to be the best that I can be. I want to do and have
and live in a way that is in harmony with my idea of the greatest
goodness. I want to harmonize physically here in this body with that
which I believe to be the best, or the good way, of life."

If you will make those statements, and then do not take action
unless you feel good, you will always be moving upon the path
in harmony with your idea of that which is good.
—Abraham, as channeled by Ester Hicks

O n many evenings our family had lively discussions about
God, the role faith played in one's life, and the importance of
believing in the hereafter.

Dan often took the lead in the discussions. It became evident that
he had a firm understanding of his beliefs, what the church was all about
in individuals' lives, and how it affected the people in our community.
After his confirmation, however, Dan started to show signs of fatigue. We
wondered what that meant.

After so many months of relative calm we were taken aback when the
Mayo Clinic called and said there was a problem. They requested that we
come to the clinic for a meeting with the oncologists.

We sat and listened as they explained to us there was some concern
early on that all of the cancer might not have been caught during Dan's

initial surgery as everyone had hoped. The cruel reality was that the cancer had metastasized to Dan's lungs.

Not good. Not good at all.

His regular checkup revealed that he now had a series of small, and a couple of larger tumors in his lungs. Evidently, the three types of chemotherapy he had been taking were no longer effective for the type of cancer he had.

The discussion centered on another approach, namely that we consider a course of experimental drugs. We met as a family with the oncologists and explored the options. We also made it clear to Dan that the decision was his and we weren't going to insist on anything *for* him. He had the right to make the decision and we would support anything he decided to do. He chose to take the protocol of the experimental drugs.

We made numerous trips from our home in Winona to the Mayo Clinic in Rochester, Minnesota, which was a forty-five-mile trip through Minnesota farm country. As that treatment continued for four or five months, the time seemed to drag on.

The intense treatments Dan endured took their toll on him. He had difficulty sleeping and eating, and his physical deterioration was easy to see.

The weekends brought some relief, as he didn't have treatments then and could catch up on sleep and regain some of his appetite.

At one of Dan's weekly consultations with the oncologists, my wife and I were called into the little office situated on the floor where all of the other children received their treatment. The doctor, who'd become very fond of Dan in his fight to beat the cancer, looked somber. I sensed immediately that the news wasn't going to be good.

He looked at us. "I'm sorry, but Dan's run out of options. The treatment isn't working and continuing these drugs will probably do more harm than good. There just isn't anything else we can do for him. Take him home."

We were in shock. I remember saying to myself, *What exactly does that mean, take Dan home? Of course, we'll take Dan home, like we've been doing for the past two years.*

We went home.

* * *

Still clueless, the next day I asked Grace when Dan's next scheduled appointment was. She said she didn't know because everything was so vague.

I called the clinic and talked to the receptionist and was told that no additional visits were going to be scheduled for Dan. I then asked to talk to our doctor.

He said, "We've come to the end of the line and it's now time for your family to prepare for Dan's final days at home."

I wanted to be furious, but I was numb. I didn't want to believe that the fight was over. Then and there I decided, even though the Mayo Clinic couldn't help and had in effect given up on Dan, I would do it on my own.

I would heal him through prayer, and work toward making a miracle happen. After all, I was raised Catholic and was told by both priests and nuns most of my life that if we asked in the name of Jesus, it would be done.

That became my mantra. I knew what I had to do. So, each evening Dan and I sat together and recited the Lord's Prayer and his favorite, the 23rd Psalm. Our praying eventually encompassed many other prayers as well. As father and son, we grew incredibly close.

*   *   *

Prior to the challenges we experienced with Dan's battle, I had serious reservations about my Catholic faith and the Church in particular. As a young adult I'd questioned the Church's authority over its faithful.

Truth be told, I also couldn't relate to the Church and the business of the Mass with all the sitting, standing, kneeling and such. In order to find a way to my spiritual center and bring peace and serenity into my life, I began to meditate in the morning while everyone in the house was still sleeping. This worked well on Sundays, especially because the chaos of getting four young boys ready for church and then getting them there for Sunday Mass was a major hassle.

I think many Catholics from my generation felt obligated to go to church on Sunday out of fear of committing a mortal sin. I think it was in the *Baltimore Catechism*: If we died while in the state of mortal sin (like having missed Mass on Sunday), we had an express ride to hell! It wasn't stated quite that way, of course, but the idea is the same.

We also had to face our peers, since it was necessary to be seen going to church. Nothing like a nice heavy dose of Catholic guilt to get us motivated to go to Sunday Mass.

My issues with the Catholic Church began long before that, however. As a young teenager, I seriously began to question the whole concept of mortal versus venial sin.

Venial sins are those "lesser" sins that we commit, such as when we're looking at the shape of a girl's breasts as she walks by and we say to ourselves, "Gee, those are pretty nice breasts. I sure would like to . . ."

Hey! Stop, go to confession and tell the priest what we were thinking. *Bad boy, bad boy!* I tried to live my faith as a young Catholic lad, but I grew up as a young guy with red blood coursing through my veins and had normal sexual urges. So I was left with *more* guilt.

I couldn't wrap my head around the "eating fish on Friday" idea, either. I understood the need to make a sacrifice. That seemed okay and even somewhat logical, but if I ate meat on Friday, I'd committed a venial sin. *Oh-oh.*

*   *   *

Another experience that has stayed with me all these years involves my first communion. Back then, we were not allowed to eat or drink anything for an hour before receiving communion, or the Host. So here we are, all the boys, dressed in white suits and shoes, and walking through the school hall on the way to Mass.

The kid in front of me, on the spur of the moment, decides to take a sip of water as he passes the water fountain. Bad luck for him; good ol' Sister What's-Her-Name sees him and yanks him out of the line and sends him home.

"Sister, come on, really? You have got to be kidding me!" A nine-year-old kid got busted for a sip of water. I'm *sure* he became a priest later on in life. (Pardon my sarcasm.)

Add to all of my teenage questions, the whole bit about contraception for married couples, and I was a Catholic with some very serious doubts about the Church.

In the '60s, contraception was a big deal for young Catholic couples. The Church could basically tell us when we could or couldn't enjoy a physical relationship with our spouse. We had to have rhythm, of course. If our spouse wasn't so good at calculating the days relating to her ovulation time, we were in trouble. And if, on the off chance pregnancy resulted, well then, it was "good girl, good boy," and the Church was pleased. We were supposed to accept that it was God's will.

Oh, and by the way, we could offer a financial gift which allowed us to buy indulgences as a way of lessening our venial sins, at least.

Reflection: *For some, organized religion is a sure path to their salvation . . . and that's fine. For others, finding a spiritual path away from a church, temple, or mosque is also very good. In "A Course in Miracles" it states that there are over 1,000 paths to find your way to God. The key, it seems, is to find the path that is best for you.*

I was faced with a serious dilemma. On the one hand, I was no longer connected with the Church of my youth on either an emotional or spiritual level, and yet I needed a basis from which to launch a major prayer effort to help save Dan. My hope for a cure and my deep and abiding faith in God were never shaken; in fact they were rock solid, but all of my prayers were sourced in the Church.

See, I hadn't yet gained the level of spiritual awareness to communicate with my spirit guides, to ask for guidance and direction. So at that juncture, practiced, traditional Catholic prayer took on a whole new level of meaning . . . all of a sudden the stakes were incredibly high.

I wanted a miracle. I wanted to save Dan, and I wanted my Catholic faith and my Church to help me do it.

* * *

The conundrum was that I was once very connected with my Catholic faith. I had in fact "bought the farm" when I was a young teenager. I believed most of everything I heard and learned back then.

But in this time of trying to do the right thing through my praying with Dan, I missed an important part of the reality of what was really occurring.

Mr. John Piper, of the Desiring God organization, has shed some light on it for me with this profound message:

"When you read the word 'hope' in the Bible (1 Peter 1:13), set your 'hope' fully on the grace that will be brought to you at the revelation of Jesus Christ. So hope is not wishful thinking. It's not, 'I don't know if it's going to happen, but I hope it happens.' That is absolutely not what is meant by Christian faith. Christian hope is when God has promised that something is going to happen and you put your trust in that promise. Christian hope is a confidence that something will come to pass because God has promised it will come to pass. Hope is a portion or part of faith. Faith and hope, in my mind, are overlapping realities; hope is faith in the future tense. So, most of faith is hope."

Reflection: Without hope, life would be empty and seemingly without meaning. Hoping for an outcome to something drives us toward the end result we desire even if, unbeknownst to us, the outcome is not what we had hoped for.

The experience of losing a child is devastating. What made it worse for me was that I chose to believe that it was a horrific experience and my ego was completely caught up in the grief. In the aftermath of Dan's passing, my life was riddled with and dominated by anger. I was full of rage and felt abandoned by God.

As I gained knowledge of the reality of the spirit world, my perception of what happens on earth during our incarnation here is just as those words from *A Course in Miracles* point out. "There is another way of looking at the world," and this is what I choose to believe now.

I simply do not, and cannot, have all the information as it relates to the situation. I also believe at some point I really and truly will understand what it all meant.

* * *

Therein is the reality of my entire experience with trying to save Dan. The experience of praying with Dan as he went through his battle with cancer was steeped in hope. But, it was *my* hope. I thought if I prayed enough, sincerely enough, strong enough, often enough, then Dan would be cured. The part I wasn't aware of is that Dan had *his* own reality. He was on *his* journey and was in fact fulfilling *his* purpose in this lifetime. It was never about me even though I thought back then I had the power to change his destiny.

*   *   *

A Course in Miracles provided truthful, sobering information, and with it came the realization that a part of recovery, be it from alcoholism or grieving the loss of a loved one, is our awareness of how dominating and powerful our egos are relative to how we think and, thus, how we feel about the world around us.

Living with a sick child is profound for any parent. Learning that I actually had a choice in how I perceived what was actually taking place was a real eye-opener for me. Without knowing any of that, I chose to drive the situation out of fear, with a forceful egotism that demanded the miracle of physical healing.

As I have journeyed on, I have come to understand on a deeper spiritual level how we are connected to the spirit world. Spiritualists, philosophers, and others suggest that a thin veil exists between our world and the spirit world.

In his book, *The Seat of the Soul*, Gary Zukav refers to the connection we have with the spirit world prior to our incarnation into this existence. Similarly, others have postulated that we do indeed choose our parents, we choose the path we will be on, and that we also have an agreement about the purpose our lives will fulfill while we are here in this life.

The following is a thought from Gary Zukav on the subject:

"If a child dies early in its life, we do not know what agreement was made between that child's soul and the soul of its parents, or

what healing was served by that experience. Although we are sympathetic to the anguish of the parents, we cannot judge this event. If we, or the parents of that child, do not understand the impersonal nature of the dynamic that is in motion, we may react with anger towards the Universe, or towards each other, or with guilt if we feel that our actions were inadequate. All of these reactions create karma, and more lessons for the soul to learn—more karmic debts for the soul to pay—appear."

So how did it all play out in the end, when Dan made his final transition into the spirit world? I believe now and embrace the reality that Dan had a reason to experience everything he lived through while he was here dancing on this earth, just as we have our own unique purpose as we dance on this earth for the time we have to do so.

And by the way, back then I would not have used the term "transition into the spirit world" as another way of saying that someone had died. My belief now is that use of the transition phrase speaks to a deeper understanding of faith and what our own purpose in this incarnation means for each of us.

Was all the praying that we did for nothing? Today, I don't believe that to be true. Was I naïve in thinking that I had the power to change Dan's destiny because that's what I wanted? Yes, without a doubt.

Should people stop praying for a miracle to happen when times are difficult? Absolutely not! Why? Because praying is a distinct series of events that mirror the love you have for someone. The outpouring of prayer is an outpouring of love, and love is the most powerful element of our human existence.

Dan came to us and, in his short fifteen years on this earth, left a legacy of how one can find himself and grow to have a deep and abiding faith in life with God, his family, and in understanding that the spirit world is closer to each of us than we know.

Sharing Dan's life while he was here has been a blessing too large for words. He gave me the opportunity to reinvent myself into a person who has been extremely successful in business, and who has a sincere willingness to help others. Today I enjoy a sense of peacefulness and harmony that I never would have imagined possible.

*   *   *

The following is an excerpt from the book *Simple and Profound,* from the Joseph Collective of spirit guides, channeled through Susan Burns, with editorial guidance from Judith Struck.

How is forgiveness a part of healing?

Have you ever noticed how angry some people get when they are experiencing a difficulty? They want to blame and lash out at something or someone. Their anger usually comes from the fear of the unknown that is created by the difficulty. If they can accept that the difficulty is an experience that will contribute to their growth, they will deal with it much better. They can do this acceptance easily if they do not look at the problem as the enemy but as the opportunity. So by forgiving the problem for disturbing their lives and accepting that the problem is bringing growth, healing begins.

To be honest, it was years before I understood the message from Joseph. I now see the experience of losing Dan as gaining an understanding of the magnificence that he was and the magnificence of who I am.

Helen Reddy says it best in her song titled *"I Am Woman."* In it she sings: "Yes, I am wise, but it is wisdom born of pain. Yes, I've paid the price, but look how much I've gained."

And that is what I believe as well . . . what I have experienced has been painful, but I am so much wiser and have a level of understanding that brings with it, untold peace.

Chapter Five

Conversations

"We must never forget that we may also find meaning in life even when confronted with a hopeless situation, when facing a fate that cannot be changed. For what then matters is to bear witness to the uniquely human potential at its best, which is to transform a personal tragedy into a triumph, to turn one's predicament into a human achievement."
—Viktor Frankl, *Man's Search for Meaning*

During the last months of Dan's time with us a number of events occurred that, to this day, have special meaning as significantly powerful events.

On one of the trips to the Mayo Clinic, Dan was resting in the backseat of the car, with his mom driving. She said he casually mentioned that the night before this particular trip he hadn't been able to sleep. Whether he dreamt it or not, he said, a figure he thought was an angel stood by his bed, surrounded by a faint white light.

He thought it was around three o'clock in the morning. Then the angel spoke to him briefly, saying that he came to tell Dan that "No matter what happens, I will be with you, no matter what."

No one in our family knew what to make of that experience and we were awestruck. Did it really happen?

As Dan mentioned many times, it could very well have been a dream. He did say, however, that it brought great comfort to him and made him feel safe. As the months slowly rolled by, a number of our adult friends and many of Dan's classmates came by the house to visit with him. People would often say how sorry they were that he had to go through all of what he'd been experiencing.

*   *   *

I overheard some uncanny conversations between Dan and some of our adult friends while I fixed refreshments for them.

I was always awestruck to hear him tell his visitors time and time again, "I don't know why, but I have a good sense that there is a reason for this."

Sometimes he'd say, "There is an answer, I just don't know what it is yet."

I couldn't believe my ears. Even knowing there was no longer any medical assistance for him, our fifteen-year-old had insight at a level beyond his young age.

It was an enlightening time for me because I didn't expect such profound words to come from my son. Many times when his visitors were gone, he would sit on the edge of the sofa in the living room with his hands tucked under his chin and slowly rock side to side. He looked pensive.

The first time I saw him sitting there, I was afraid to ask him anything. I tried several times to find out what he needed or if I could help him in any way, but he would simply say, "No, I'm just thinking."

In the ensuing weeks we had several conversations, but they were limited in depth mainly because I wasn't at a place where I had given up hope for the miracle that would save him. I was still convinced there was a chance he could be healed. After all, we were both still praying together. And I believed I would get what I wanted if I prayed enough.

In retrospect I understand now that Dan was processing, to some degree, the inevitable. I wasn't even close to that level of awareness. I believe he had a better sense of the outcome than I did.

*   *   *

One of the most profound discussions that Dan and I had came on a Saturday night about three months prior to his passing. The boys were going through their bath routines and Dan was the last to finish in the tub and get ready for bed. He dawdled for a while in the bath, and I asked

37

him to hurry up because everyone else was getting settled in their rooms for the night and it was getting late.

I asked if everything was okay and if was he all right. He responded that everything was good, but he also said, rather briskly, that I needed to give him some space. I could tell he was irritated with me, or at something, because his responses were pretty snappy, which was unlike him.

So I told him I was going into my room to read, and if he needed anything he could come and find me there. After about twenty minutes, he finally emerged from the bathroom, came into my room, and sat at the foot of the bed.

For three or four minutes he sat there not saying anything. With his eyes downcast, he seemed to be deep in thought. I asked what was troubling him.

"Dad, do you remember the sermon that Father John gave during one of the Sunday Masses we attended about two years ago at Saint Mary's College?" he asked.

I said, "Yes, I remember it."

"Ya know," he said, "the gist of the story was that each person had the free will to make choices in his or her life. They could choose to lead a life similar to that of being a grain of sand, staying on the beach, with other grains of sand in a rather inert position and place. And that for all intents and purposes, the grain of sand was just there taking up space.

"Or," he said, "a person could choose to be like a blade of grass: vibrant, green, and growing, and full of the sun's life-giving energy."

He looked at me. "In the sermon, Father John's story was that the blade of grass was among other blades of grass, supporting the earth with their color and beauty. They shared their gifts with the world. Then, when its days were completed, it fell back to the earth after having shared its life and giving its beauty to all those who could see it and, from that point in its existence, it blended back into the soil, giving of itself to nurture and assist all the other blades of grass that would follow in its place."

Dan took a deep breath. "That blade of grass was alive and shone brightly in the sun, and then it passed on as it offered nourishment to the next generation of hearty blades of grass."

I wasn't sure where he was going, but I acknowledged that I did remember the sermon very well and mentioned I was surprised he remembered it so well.

He looked at me for several moments, and then said in a halting voice, "Dad, I am so sad and disappointed that I won't get to be like a blade of grass. I just won't be able to let my light shine as long as I wanted to. I won't be able to live my life and share the gifts that I know I have."

We sat there looking at each other in silence. I was stunned. Not knowing what to say, I got up from the bed and put my arm around him and said that we still had time to work for the miracle. We would never give up trying for him, that he had the support of all of us in our family.

That night, sleep did not come. My mind was in a swirl, my rage at God building as the unfairness of the situation became more and more real. The whole thing was out of control. I was helpless, and that thought hurt—deep down it festered.

The journey continued for Dan and his body became weaker. I gave up my company and stayed at home as Dan's primary caregiver. His mother was always present as well. His pediatrician, Dr. Joseph Repice, was able to commandeer a hospital bed for us, and allowed us to set it up in Dan's room. It became a hospice room. He was in an oxygen tent and was having trouble breathing. He didn't want to eat much.

We continued our prayer sessions, although he was no longer actively involved in them as he had been in the past. I recited the prayers and he said "Thank you." Then he requested that I read some of his favorite stories to him. One of those was the whole *Tarzan of the Apes* series. As usual, he loved to hear music. The Dan Fogelberg song, "Longer Than," was his favorite. He always got excited and smiled when that song played.

As a family, we seemed to be in a free fall. We were present to Dan, very present in fact, but we were helpless. Still I clung to the hope that it could change in a matter of days. The miracle could still manifest itself, if not instantly, certainly quickly enough to give Dan his life back. When Dan became incontinent, I remember thinking that was not a good sign.

How could God let this happen to such a great kid who had so much to give? It couldn't be the end for Dan. Yet no matter how much I raged or prayed, he continued to decline.

And that was how I happened to be sleeping on the floor next to Dan's bed on that Friday night. Tim and I woke the rest of the family, and we gathered by Dan's bedside. We cried and we prayed for Dan's safe journey into the spirit world.

*   *   *

For me, I see now, the "blade of grass" idea speaks to our desire to have a meaningful purpose in life. Purpose in life is a result of our commitment to provide substance to that which we do with our lives. I believe that's what our free will allows.

Several days later, a card came from a friend, reading: *"A brave young warrior has left the field of life. He fought long and hard and he fought well. He is a champion, and he will be missed."*

Dan did indeed fight the good fight. And, yes, we do miss him, but we also know that he walks with us.

Chapter Six

Transitions

Be not afraid.
I go before you always.
Come follow me, and
I will give you rest.
Lyrics to "Be Not Afraid," by John Michael Talbot

Dan made his transition into the spirit world shortly after midnight on July 19, 1980.

As I lay in bed the following day, I looked for meaning in our loss. It seemed as though one minute I had a son fighting for his life, hopeful that a miracle would turn things around, and then in less than a matter of a heartbeat our son was gone. Seven hours had passed, and I couldn't even begin to get a grasp of what I felt. Everything seemed to stand still. I felt numb, sort of blank. I knew where I was and was aware of my surroundings, but life seemed so different because something tragic had happened to our family. I knew my life would never be the same.

Only thing was, I wasn't sure what that meant. How different would my life be and for how long? What were the ramifications for our whole family? How would my wife and my other sons deal with it? How would people react to the news?

There were so many questions, such incredible sadness, and no answers. I felt stuck and I didn't like it. I didn't want it, but there it was. And there was nowhere to go.

The sun came up, and I finally made it out of bed with thoughts about the day ahead. To the calls that had to be made to tell the rest of our family and our friends that Dan had passed. To the arrangements for the wake and the funeral.

So many ideas swirled in my head as I headed for the shower. I wondered how everyone else in the family was holding up after what we'd experienced the night before. As it turned out, after talking to the boys and my wife, we all seemed to be in the same frame of mind . . . unable to believe that Dan's struggles were over.

Sadness and confusion invaded our household as we tried to deal with the reality. Did Dan really die? Was he in a better place? Of course, we wanted to believe he was in a better place, but believing that and not having Dan with us anymore were two different aspects to deal with.

I finally climbed in the shower and the hot water brought some comfort. As I stood under the water, my thoughts swirled again around the list of things to do.

Then, out of nowhere, I thought I heard Dan's voice: "Dad, I'm okay. Don't worry, it's all right and I'm okay."

I freaked out, got the chills, and felt totally spooked. I peeked around the shower curtain to see if someone was talking to me outside the shower, but no one was there. I thought for sure my mind was playing tricks on me because of the lack of sleep and the trauma.

At breakfast, I mentioned my Dan encounter in the shower.

Grace said, "Well, that's interesting. I heard Dan saying something similar to that while I was in the shower downstairs."

We looked at each other and I suggested that maybe we were both traumatized enough to be imagining things.

"No, Hank. I believe that was Dan's way of letting us know that he really is okay."

Everyone took great comfort in that explanation.

*   *   *

As I mentioned above, we all believed that Dan crossed over around midnight the previous night. Sometime around one o'clock in the morning of that same day and in a different part of the city, the horn in a van started blaring.

It wouldn't shut off until the owner rose from his bed and went out to the van, unlocked it, and was able to disengage it to stop the noise. The van's owner, Bud Baechler, was confused as to why the horn went off so early in the morning, especially since there were no vandals around and no rain or storms present.

He didn't have an explanation as to why the horn turned itself on. We did come up with an explanation a couple of days later. We think it had to do with the fact that during the two years that Dan fought his battle with cancer, he and Bud had become great friends.

Bud and his wife, Becky, came from musically gifted families. Using a hi-tech recording studio as a part of his work, Bud produced some of the most creative radio ads people in our part of Minnesota had ever heard.

Dan was active with his musical talent during those years, so it was natural that Dan would be invited by Bud to go to his studio to see how he created all those great radio spots. A lasting friendship and bond existed between them.

It came as no surprise to us when Bud said, "You know what I think? I think Dan just needed a way to say good-bye. As he was making his way over, he decided he'd drop a little memento and make sure that I woke up as he sped on by."

We all agreed with him.

Dan had a gift of making friends easily, primarily because he had such a great sense of humor. Our family dentist, Dr. Bob, was one of those adults Dan joked around with.

Dan could talk like Donald Duck, and you could understand what he was saying when he talked that way, which made it all the more hilarious. Dr. Bob had a special way of communicating with his young patients using humor, and he mentioned several times that he loved it whenever Dan came for his dental appointments.

We smiled when Dr. Bob's wife, Cathy, told us the following day, that she'd seen Dan at the foot of the bed in their house the night before. She said that she was awakened because she'd become chilly.

I asked her what time she thought that might have been, and she said, "Probably around two o'clock in the morning."

We all agreed that Dan was "making the rounds"—saying good-bye to some of his friends—and that included Dr. Bob.

Each of those experiences gave us great comfort. The spirit world must truly exist if, when a person "passes over," they can offer a measure of comfort to those on this side who are grieving for them.

*   *   *

Dan's body was in the capable hands of a friend, O.J., from the Fawcett Funeral Home in Winona.

After the prayer service and the hymn singing, we had the customary receiving line and did our best to minister to those who came by to pay their respects. It was particularly difficult because several grown men, fellows I knew from the YMCA, walked by the casket and upon seeing Dan in the casket, began to sob.

They wanted to say something meaningful to us but couldn't find the words. We reached out to give them comfort, which is a marvel unto itself, because I don't know where the strength came from. It was as though I was buoyed up with energy and almost outside of my body.

It wasn't easy, however. One woman came by who was a member of the Charismatic Pentecostal group from our church. She had come to the house when Dan was in his final months and performed a "laying on of hands" for his healing.

As she came to us, she said to me, "Hank, I know that you hoped Dan would be healed and would still be here, but you know, he has been healed, only in a different way."

I froze. My compassion and my ability to minister to people evaporated in a heartbeat. I wanted to strangle her because her comment made me angry. I couldn't hear what she was saying. While my exterior composure remained intact, in my mind I was screaming; I didn't think she knew what she was talking about. Now I know she was trying her best to comfort me.

The following day, the funeral Mass was held at Saint Mary's College, and thanks to Brother Peter Clifford, the president of Saint Mary's, we had a beautiful Mass service.

Even now, with so much time passed, I can still remember one of the hymns that played as we left the church. Bright sun cascaded through the stained-glass windows and the organist played the hymn, "Be Not Afraid," written by a Jesuit. I can't remember all of the words, but it starts out with, "Be not afraid, I go before you, come follow me."

To this day, whenever I hear that hymn, I flash back to that exact time, that day, that event . . . instantly.

* * *

The burial at Woodlawn Cemetery was attended by many of Dan's classmates and family friends. It was a beautiful day and, like so many experiences, it offered up a special scene for us to remember.

The sun shone and Dan's resting place was beneath a majestic maple tree. As the casket was about to be lowered, a single monarch butterfly flitted around the top of the casket and landed on top of it. We all looked on in pleasant surprise as it stayed there. Needless to say, the monarch butterfly is our reminder of Dan.

And so, as the reality of Dan's passing started to seep in, I began to get in touch with my true feelings. I took his passing as a personal failure because I hadn't been able to prevent his death, and I blamed God for allowing it.

I had a sense that the rest of my journey wasn't going to be pretty, because I was harboring strong feelings of disappointment and rage toward God.

My conversations with God occurred as soon as I woke in the morning. Remembering who I was and what my lot in life entailed, hurt deeply.

Alone late at night, I would again revisit my mistrust in God. When I went out for a long run (jogging) through the countryside of southern Minnesota, God and I had many intimate conversations, albeit only one-way. I demanded to know, over and over again (actually shouting), how

He could let such a tragedy happen to our family. We were devoted, good people. Why us? Why Dan? The more I raged, the angrier I became.

After all the praying that Dan and I'd done, I said, "Hey, wait just a flipping minute, you have got to be kidding me. When I tried so hard to prevent Dan's death from happening, you allowed it!"

What happened to the old *Baltimore Catechism*? Who is God? *God is love!* So I reminded God (daily and with great passion) that He'd screwed up big-time. I also mentioned that it appeared we had a very serious communication problem.

I repeatedly asked myself what I should or could have done differently in my life to prevent the death of my son. I beat on myself constantly.

Might I have been a better person if, for instance, I went to church more often? Maybe this was God's way of showing me that doubting my faith wasn't a good thing to do.

Was I really an egoistic guy, too full of myself?

The guilt was pervasive and debilitating. I slipped into a morass of self-deprecating angst, the despair fueled by ever-increasing guilt, and I couldn't shut it down.

The interesting thing is, people began to unwittingly feed into the self-pity that I wanted to get away from, even though I didn't realize I was feeling sorry for myself.

Whenever I met my running buddies at the local sports bar after running hard miles over the noon hour, other friends would come to me and put their hand on my shoulder and say how sorry they were to hear about Dan's passing. Before I knew it, a pitcher of beer would be put on the table where I was sitting. The scenario was repeated time and again.

Well, someone had to drink all that beer, and I was willing to do it. I didn't even realize that my drinking was out of control.

Memory flashback: I remember the early years of growing up in my family, where drinking was a popular social activity. The more I drank now, the more I recalled that a couple of my uncles drank to excess whenever we had parties at our house. I did know, firsthand, that my mother very likely had a drinking problem, but I never "connected the dots" that I too might have a potential drinking problem. I found out I did have alcoholism in my genes. Later on in this book, I share several experiences about the treatment center that I attended in Minnesota. But suffice it to say, the revelation is that there is as much alcohol in a bottle of beer as in a shot of whiskey! I didn't know that back then.

Statistically, that became significant because I thought with all the daily running and the fact that I restricted my drinking to beer only, I was safe from having a problem. My rationale to drink, of course, was that all runners, especially those who were running sixty to sixty-five miles a week as I was doing, ought to replace those lost electrolytes and, in my mind, beer qualified as the "electrolyte replacement beverage" of choice.

New business opportunities allowed me to expand my expertise of service, which encompassed the raising of funds for nonprofit organizations such as colleges and agencies, and building functional development and fund-raising offices. I also assisted with marketing an electronics firm that manufactured proprietary electronic machines. Dan R., the president of the firm, was a friend and an excellent mentor in bringing me into the electronics industry. Much of my time demanded travel, and at first it didn't seem to make much of a difference. But eventually, as I continued to battle the anger I felt toward God, the demons came a-calling. I ran and exercised every day. I drank as much (replacing those lost electrolytes, of course), if not more that I ran.

*   *   *

I struggled constantly with my anger toward God and couldn't get beyond it. It felt good to dump on God.

That anger was heightened when my wife and I met people in various stores about town. Most folks didn't know what to say to us. Others ignored us as though we had the plague.

One time I was pushing a grocery cart in the supermarket, and as I came down one of the aisles, some folks we knew came around the same aisle at the far end. When they saw me, they abruptly turned around and scooted down the aisle on the other side of the store.

Feeling sorry for myself, as I mentioned earlier, came easily since it seemed as though all of our friends felt that way toward us. The more I felt sorry for myself, the more I continued to run and drink. Without a doubt I was running to release the anger that was eating me up inside. It's a wonder I didn't get sick from all the venom I had inside me.

These seemingly small things added up to a tipping point that came when we had our first Thanksgiving without Dan.

Prior to that year I'd always had a profound sense of thankfulness, as our family was healthy, happy, and blessed. Not so the year Dan died, though.

I remember, as I said grace before the meal, I almost choked on the words. "Dear Lord, we thank you for all the blessings we have as a family."

In fact, that sort of ended it for me right there. We made it through the Thanksgiving meal, albeit in a somber mood.

That next Sunday, I went to church by myself and a dear priest friend of mine, Father Paul, was saying Mass at the chapel at Saint Mary's College where I worked. Flooded by thoughts of disappointment and severely deranged with anger, I couldn't sit and listen any longer to what Father Paul was saying.

I got up from the pew and left the church. *This is all total bullshit and I don't need any of it,* I said to myself.

I experienced a major faith crisis. God and I were no longer on speaking terms.

* * *

Many friends rallied around and tried hard to help us through the grieving process. Some friends didn't know what to say to us while others called to see how we were doing with it all.

One such friend gave me a book titled *On Death and Dying*, written by the Swiss psychiatrist, Elisabeth Kübler-Ross.

Her research explains five stages of the grieving process, which are:

Phase 1. Denial – It was fairly easy to move beyond this phase since the doctor at the Mayo Clinic spelled it out clearly.

Phase 2. Anger – This phase was my biggest hurdle to overcome. My profound feelings of anger and mistrust went beyond anything I had ever experienced before in my life. God was the recipient of the rage.

Phase 3. Bargaining – I tried at one point to make a trade with God. Take me instead of my son. It doesn't work that way.

Phase 4. Depression – Without all the running and jogging that I did, I would be in the loony bin as we speak.

Phase 5. Acceptance – At long last, the truth of it emerged. I came to have some understanding of what life is all about. I'm quick to add, however, that I'm still learning.

I found the whole idea of what Dr. Kübler-Ross was proposing helpful. I learned that the stages do not necessarily follow one after the other. They can be switched around and can repeat themselves.

Good to know, I thought.

As it turned out, my denial stage involved a short span of time. My bargaining period was a little longer as I tried to convince God to take me instead of Dan, but to no avail. To say that I was depressed is an understatement, but I covered it up with anger. Acceptance did come, but not until years had passed and not until I was finally ready to give in and let my anger toward God fall away. The anger stage was the most difficult one for me to overcome.

I became bitter and resentful and my anger allowed me to wallow in self-pity . . . all the while directing my ill will toward the only one who I believed deserved it—God.

*   *   *

The months of traveling around the countryside seemed to fly by, and I was drinking and running, running and drinking.

Finally, several very concerned friends started to talk to me. They had the courage to let me know they didn't like my behavior, and some even told me they wanted me to take a good honest look at what I was doing with my life.

In retrospect, I can understand now how much they truly cared for me and my family. During those days my marriage was beginning to fray. Obviously, my drinking added fuel to the fire of discontent. When I visited the Ronald McDonald House in Rochester, MN, one day, I heard that 85 percent of the couples who lose a child will split up. I was shocked by that statistic. It seemed awfully high. I mentioned it to my wife, and we decided that it would be best to prevent anything like that with some marriage counseling.

Individual counseling made sense to me too, and I relied on Father John, who was a professional counselor as well as a Catholic priest. He served as the chaplain at a college in Winona. One day we met for about three hours, and his purpose was to convince me to seek professional help through Alcoholics Anonymous and enroll in the A.A. Twelve Step Program.

We argued throughout that session. I held the position that nothing was wrong and I could slow down my drinking on my own. He argued that I was full of myself and overwhelmed by my outlandish ego. He stressed that I needed help, big-time.

If you haven't ever had a priest stand up to you and in terms that would make a truck driver blush, then you haven't lived. He won the argument, and I told him I would check out the possibilities of getting professional help.

A day later, Dan R., the president of EMT Electronics, called me into his office for "a chat." As I took a seat in front of his desk he told me he was really concerned for me and my family. He said that several of his engineers with whom I traveled to promote his products, mentioned to him that I could really consume beer, and at a major-league level. They were concerned.

With tears in his eyes, he said he loved me as a dear friend and wanted me to seek professional help to change my life. He said it looked very much as though I was in trouble, and that I myself couldn't or wouldn't see it.

Wow—two days in a row and a double whammy about getting help. Getting help was now number one on my agenda.

* * *

I called another friend in Minneapolis who I knew was an A.A. counselor in private practice, Brother Bill. He was a Christian Brother from Saint Mary's College, and he said he'd look into getting me information about one of the best treatment centers in the country, Hazelden, located in Center City, MN, north of Saint Paul.

The information came to me several days later, and he said he could pull a few strings and have me admitted in a couple of weeks. I panicked.

This was moving way too quickly. Besides, my insurance only covered a third of the cost, so I would need $1,800 to be admitted to Hazelden. My wife and I figured out we could come up with about $800 of the cost of admittance.

On one hand, I felt relieved I couldn't go to Hazelden. Then very late one night, when everyone was in bed and the house was quiet, I got to thinking that deep down inside I really knew something wasn't right with all the drinking.

I decided I did want to get help, but the stumbling block of not having the money was too much for me. I started feeling sorry for myself and again asked God for help. I must admit my level of trust in God was at an all-time minimum. However, the pain and fear I felt were overwhelming. So, without any fancy plan or fancy prayers, I simply asked God for help.

Please let there be a way for me to get help.

I slumped onto a chair in the recreation room downstairs, completely exhausted and overwhelmed by shame and guilt. Feeling alone and adrift, I started to sob.

I hit the bottom of an emotional roller coaster, feeling I had no one to turn to and nowhere to go. I needed help and finally knew it. My pride and ego stuffed away, I sat there in the dark room and called out, repeating the words over and over: "Dear God, I need help, I need help."

Eventually I dozed off.

The next day seemed like every other day, with the exception that I'd made a personal commitment to myself to change my life. If I couldn't come up with the money to get into the treatment center, then I would find a Twelve Step Program.

Late that afternoon I received a call from Bud. He asked if I would stop by his house because he had a few things he wanted to run by me. We'd been working together on a couple of projects, and I had shared with him that I was thinking about going into Hazelden but didn't think it would happen without the money needed to get in.

As I was leaving his house, he and his wife, Becky, came over and gave me a hug. In the process, he tucked a folded check in my shirt pocket. He simply said, "Perhaps this will help you to get to Hazelden." As I drove down the street, I slowly pulled the check from my pocket and saw that it was for $500.

I exclaimed, "Wow, what a gift!"

The next morning I received a telephone call from Brother Raymond, a professor at Saint Mary's College, asking if I could stop by for a chat with him.

Oh-oh, another chat. When I arrived, we exchanged the usual greetings, and then he asked if I had any intention of getting help with the grief of losing a son, because he knew that I was really struggling.

I told him of my plan to try to get into Hazelden. He said he was delighted to hear that and reached in his desk drawer and proceeded to hand me a folded check. He said his family had a foundation and some money to give away for a special purpose. I was floored. I thanked him and told him I would keep in touch regarding my progress. As I drove home I reached into my pocket and saw a check for $500.

Hazelden, here I come.

* * *

By the way, I asked Brother Raymond if he had talked to Bud before our meeting and he said that he hadn't spoken to Bud in months. Go figure.

Reflection: *There are no coincidences in life. Events happen for a reason. It is easy to doubt or dismiss that idea; however, time and time again, I have witnessed situations that have been awe inspiring.*

* * *

Prior to my leaving for Hazelden, I stopped by the rectory to let Father John know I was on my way. He handed me a book titled *Love Is Letting Go of Fear*, by Dr. Gerald Jampolsky. It's a marvelous introduction into the study and basic concepts of *A Course in Miracles*.

I highly recommend it as a spiritual path of awakening. It proved to be a great beginning for me, and opened the door into the bigger and more complete study of *A Course in Miracles*, which allows one to grasp the role the ego plays in our thinking. It also opens a way to come to know the meaning of love and forgiveness in our lives.

A quote from *A Course in Miracles* states: "Trials are but lessons that you failed to learn presented once again, so where you made a faulty choice before, you now can make a better one, and thus escape all pain that what you chose before has brought to you."

Chapter Seven
One Step Toward Freedom

"When you are on a journey, it is certainly helpful to know where you are going or at least the general direction in which you are moving, but don't forget: the only thing that is ultimately real about your journey is the step that you are taking at this moment. That's all there is."
—Eckhart Tolle, from *The Power of Now*

T he thirty-day program at Hazelden was incredible. I learned about the disease of alcoholism and was faced with the constant challenge to look at my family background and the dynamics that I experienced both as a youngster and as an adult.

The "personal inventory" process in itself was an eye-opener. I was asked to review as many life experiences as I could remember regarding the relationship aspects of my parents and aunts and uncles. Probing questions centered on how alcohol was used or abused in my family. Success in this process was based on being honest. It seemed relatively easy to protect my family by not revealing all the things that took place over the years; however, Hazelden professionals are trained to sift through what is being revealed and what is not being revealed. Without honesty, there was no chance for success in recovery.

* * *

The group I was assigned to consisted of, on average, ten men called the Cronin Group, named after the building we were in. Several attendees were repeating the program while others, like me, were first timers.

The mix proved rather interesting because those who were repeating the experience, when asked to share their stories in the group sessions, were great teachers. They explained why and how they "slipped" (which means they started to drink again). Their honesty was sincere and allowed the rest of us to gain great insight as to where and how the pitfalls could occur once we'd left the program and returned to the "real" world.

Memory flashback: There were several profound experiences for me, and one was a talk I had with my first roommate. Hal, who was a dozen years my senior, was back for his fourth tour at Hazelden. If anyone wonders about whether or not the Holy Spirit is alive and well and lives among us, this story might help in understanding that concept.

I was in Hazelden because I couldn't deal with the grief of losing my son, and I drank to excess to mask it. Hal was back because he couldn't deal with the grief of losing a son also.

Our talks lasted into the wee hours of the morning and were inspiring events for me. One night he shared with me that the biggest reason he kept on drinking was because he couldn't find a way to finally bury his son and move on with his life. He suggested that I'd better find a way to bury my son, Dan, or else I would probably face relapses, too. At first I thought it interesting that my first roommate would be someone who lost a son as well.

In Alcoholics Anonymous, several sayings are considered gospel to those of us in recovery: Keep it simple; Don't overanalyze things; One day at a time. I would add another: There are no coincidences in life. I was destined to share some time with Hal, and he proved to be a great teacher.

Another fellow who kept coming back for return visits was Jim from Chicago. On his third trip back, he finally admitted that whenever he left treatment and went back home, it was always a return into the same family and job dynamics that had caused the problem in the first place.

Counselors often advised him that, when leaving Hazelden, perhaps he should pay attention to those dynamics as they undoubtedly created a potential for disaster. He explained the scenario: He would walk home from the train station after work and pass by the same bar where he used to stop for a "before-dinner drink." So he would stop and have one drink. Then when he arrived home, his wife would question him as to why he stopped at the bar. With no good reason, his only defense was to argue that "he could handle it." That proved to be his downfall each and every time he left treatment.

The important lesson I learned from that story about Jim was the understanding that things leading you down the path of unhealthy behavior need to be avoided—at all costs—if you are going to be successful in your recovery.

However, knowing and understanding this concept might point out that the relationship you are in is toxic and does more harm to you than good. The other side of the argument is, of course, that you have to examine yourself first and get a very good grip on what your own foibles are before you blame your partner as the cause of your problems.

Reflection: It is unfair to judge people based on what you see, i.e., how they look, the clothes they wear, whether or not they are obese or thin, or if they have tattoos, etc. We don't have all the information as to what exactly they are going through in their lives, so it seems rather foolish to judge someone because we think they ought to be different. At any rate, perhaps we aren't all that great in their eyes either.

As cohorts, we spent our days in group sessions discussing all manner of topics. Mostly we shared life stories, allowing plenty of time for feedback from various members in the group. Again, the trained professionals were at their best during these times. They deftly moved the discussions to an understanding of what correct behavior looked like in different life situations.

In the evenings, each of the different groups came together for a lecture which was provided by "alumni" of the Hazelden program. A memorable lecture for me was from a fellow by the name of Ed, who talked about "King Baby Ego."

He went on to explain that most, if not all, alcoholics suffered from an outrageous sense of self-importance. In many cases it led to the crazy belief that they were above the law and could do no wrong no matter how outrageous their behavior had become. Hence, the ego was "over the top," so to speak. His favorite line, which he repeated over and over, was the mantra of the egotist: "I want what I want when I want it."

That concept immediately made sense, and I knew it would soon be my fate to deal with my ego. My hope was that I would gain some understanding of what it meant to have a healthy ego and not one that controlled the creation of self.

I learned that the ego could and would demand that it be acknowledged as the center of the universe. That "other" person living inside the same body was *not* the authentic one. Later on, as I studied *A Course in Miracles*, it became clear how the ego's defense of itself and its power compose a very real force in dominating one's life.

The spirituality of the Twelve Step Program was like a breath of fresh air. It allowed me to look and feel the way I always wanted to look and feel about my soul and who I was—FREE.

This freedom meant I was unfettered by rules demanding I understand what a bad person I am; that we are born into original sin and bad from day one of our existence. "Free" meant I was no longer bound by the concept that if I committed a sin based on the do's and don'ts of the Church, the guy in the red suit with horns on his head and carrying a spear was holding the door open for me and saying, "Welcome to the Hotel California!"

The Twelve Steps are listed in the appendix for your reference. Suffice it to say how liberating it was to relate to God in a personal way. To call God whatever I believed He or She was. That could be "God," my "Higher Power," or whatever I wanted my God to be. For me, this was the beginning of my salvation—from myself.

*   *   *

The program calls for all of its adherents to be honest. Authenticity is the goal, and with it would come sobriety. Being clean and sober, as we say in the program, allows for more days of happiness than days of despair. Gone are the games, gone are the untruths. Gone is the knowledge that it's okay to play mind games with yourself and all those around you.

The old cloak of guilt and shame is slowly washed away, and that which is revealed is a marvelous, beautiful soul. It is a time when a new soul is waiting to be nurtured and brought fully to new life. This was so exciting—so very exciting—and so life giving. *Thank you, Bill W.!* (He was the founder of A.A.)

*   *   *

It was time to leave Hazelden and begin a new life of looking at what most people call the "real" world. The task included planning for the dreams I now had, yet staying aware of the demons and all the games I had played and let others play.

And of course, the temptations that had created the negative hoopla in the first place were still present. Life became a free-for-all of feelings and fears of failing, but without any ego-inflicted grandiose ideas of my own self-importance. Stripped bare of the foolish and inflated thoughts of who I was, I no longer saw the world through rose-colored glasses. The journey to experience true healing had begun, and there was no turning back.

The Hazelden experience pointed out clearly that I'd dealt with the pain of losing Dan by drinking to excess and not facing the cold hard truth. Running away from a very difficult experience wasn't the healthy way of getting on with my life. Rather, it only put the inevitable on hold. The bottom line was: If I was going to survive the crisis, I would have to handle it differently.

My time at Hazelden offered a solution. As painful as the truth was, it paled in comparison to what I had already been through. Once you've climbed Mt. Everest, everything else coming your way are hills.

The Twelve Step Program showed me there were other issues that I had no knowledge of. These included: that I came from an alcoholic family; that I was an adult child of an alcoholic parent; that I had a strong proclivity to become an alcoholic; and with so many of my uncles exhibiting drinking problems, it was obvious that I had the disease in my genes.

*   *   *

Step 1 in the Twelve Step Program of Alcoholics Anonymous is said to be the major hurdle to whether or not a person will be successful in recovery. It states: **"We admitted we were powerless over alcohol— that our lives had become unmanageable."** In truth, it was the second part of Step 1 that hit me between the eyes, so to speak, because my life had indeed become unmanageable. I also became aware of how dominant my ego was (and still is). This realization was insightful, since it led to understanding that my ego and my drive to save my son had culminated in the thought process that I could in fact change the destiny of another person, e.g., save my son.

I know it's a normal parental reaction to want to save our children. I would guess every parent would want that. I just took it to an extreme and then experienced a severe faith crisis when the result was not what I had demanded. I never realized that I didn't have control over the situation.

It wasn't until I internalized the value of Dan's life, his purpose for being here, and the gifts he shared with all of us who knew him, that I could move forward with my life, reestablish my relationship with God, and stop blaming the Catholic Church as a part of the failure that I felt.

Memory flashback: Life's circumstances have a way of moving us ever so slowly in the direction we are intended to go, and I believe now that the Holy Spirit has had a direct hand in my transformation. As I forged ahead in building my consulting practice shortly after Dan passed over to the spirit world, I had a *chance* meeting with Sister Judith Marie Beck, SSM. I say chance meeting, but, as already mentioned, I believe strongly that things happen for a reason. Sister Judith Marie served as an administrator with the Sisters of the Sorrowful Mother (SSM), a Catholic order of religious women.

A quote from the SSM's website regarding their history states:

> *"The Sisters of the Sorrowful Mother both serve and empower*
> *the poor by sharing God's love through ministry and prayer. We are*
> *skilled teachers, compassionate caregivers, attentive counselors,*
> *caring friends and gentle companions to those in need—the sick,*

> *the poor, the young, the old and those in crisis. Inspired by St.*
> *Francis, St. Clare and our Foundress, Mother Frances Streitel,*
> *we live simply, give generously, and have a deep respect and loving*
> *concern for all of creation. Through prayer and work, we bring*
> *fuller life to others."*

No doubt about it, the Twelve Step Program was a great source of spiritual reawakening for me. The experience with the SSM group of women also gave me an understanding into the relevance and purpose of the Catholic Church. The Sisters that I met serve their God diligently, passionately, and with silent fervor through good works toward others who are in need.

My company was hired to create and produce a centennial booklet of the work of the SSM Sisters during the past 100 years, since the founding of the order by Sister Amalia Streitel in 1895. (Mother Frances Streitel was born Amalia Frances Rose Streitel.) To accomplish this, Bud and I, along with Sister Judith Marie, traveled throughout the United States visiting with and interviewing Sisters who had dedicated their lives in service to others. The Sisters we interviewed included nurses, healthcare administrators, teachers, social workers, and directors of religious education programs.

The trip expanded to include Sisters in Europe as well. The transformation for me was a realization that the Catholic Church was relevant because of the people who made it so. To listen to the stories of nuns who had lived for thirty-five to forty years in the African bush country and other parts of the world serving the uneducated, sick, and hungry was at times overwhelming. What a blessing it was to visit with these Sisters who had so much to share. Feeling the magnificence of the compassion that shone from the eyes of so many religious women was a true revelation and something to behold for me. The glow that emanated from their souls was palpable. It reminded me, and still does, of the saying, "Let your light shine in the world, for all to see."

So there it was, another understanding on my part, brought to light, so to speak, through the eyes of many beautiful souls of women who shared stories about lives dedicated to serving others. I am still awestruck that women would dedicate their lives in such a loving way to help others who have nothing but the sunshine and the rain in their lives. Talk about heroes—wow, there they are!

*   *   *

The Hazelden experience, for many who make the twenty-eight day (or longer) program, gives one a new perspective of how to live life on a daily basis—with humility and remembering to live one moment at a time.

Success in recovery from alcoholism is tied directly to attending weekly or, in some cases, daily A.A. meetings. The meetings are the lifeline, if you will, for those who struggle with making the adjustment back into society without the use of a crutch (a drug of choice) to lean on. Life looks very different when you are living in the world as a functional, useful adult who is now clean and sober. At first it seems pretty scary. It can even feel horribly lonely. A simple thing like watching Sunday afternoon football is an affront to your psyche. The beer commercials alone are enough to clearly demonstrate how our society treats the consumption of alcohol. The A.A. meetings give recovering alcoholics a place to vent, or discuss all that they're being confronted with from a society that promotes with wild abandon the use of drugs (prescription drugs, cigarettes, and alcohol are only a few).

*   *   *

I thought life would improve dramatically and immediately when I left the treatment center. After all, I had powerful new insights regarding how my poor behavior and poor choices caused untold sorrows for myself, certainly, but for others as well. I expected an instantaneous level of stability in my life to be forthcoming.

Unfortunately, that isn't how life works. I realized that drinking to excess had great merit if I wanted to live in denial and continue playing mind games with myself and others. But living in and seeing the world as a sober adult was an incredible challenge, especially after spending so many years without knowing what good, healthy, and normal behavior really looked like.

Memory flashback: Back when I was drinking and prior to going into treatment, I was on a business trip in Monterey, California. Before returning home, I took an extra day to enjoy the scenery of the California coast. It was all so alluring. I walked barefoot along the beach, jogged a bit along the coast, and talked to several older fishermen about their catches of the day. I bought a bottle of wine, some cheese and a French baguette, and made my way out on a jetty overlooking Monterey Bay. I drank the wine, ate the cheese and the bread, and with a buzz from the wine, talked to the seagulls as an incredible sunset loomed on the horizon. It was a euphoric experience.

Years later, after leaving the treatment center and when I was stone-cold sober, I bought a bottle of bubbly Perrier water, some cheese, and a French baguette. As I sat on the side of one of the bluffs overlooking the Mississippi River, I drank the Perrier, ate the cheese and bread, and watched a sunset cascading over the river.

I was bored to tears and the whole experience sucked big-time. No wine, no buzz, no euphoria. It took several years before those sunsets and sunrises became absolutely spectacular to me again. But when they did, it was authentic and those sunsets and sunrises gave back their true meaning with a richness that I had never experienced or appreciated in the past. I sensed a shift in perception and it was a worthy one.

Today, through sober eyes, sunrises and sunsets have once again become, and remain, euphoric and blissful experiences.

Reflection: *Sobriety allows one to be a part of events with purity, honesty, and authenticity. The colors are richer, the meaning is deeper, and the memories are lasting.*

As I reflect back on that time, I see my thinking was confused, steeped in allowing my ego to dictate thoughts and behavior. But things would soon change.

Part Two

Time to Change: Reinventing Myself

Chapter Eight
The Long and Winding Road

"By getting in touch and staying in touch with your deepest desires, you
can find your own magic star. By continuing to focus and feel what you
really want, you will increase your power to create your life. First in your
mind and heart and then through your actions, you will be increasingly
successful in creating what you really want."
—John Gray, from *How to Know What You Want*
and Want What You Have

S lowly the fog of unknowing began to dissipate. Thoughts of clarity
led me to the notion of transitioning my life from the person
I had been and thought I was, to someone who would see the
world differently through established and accepted behaviors that were
healthy.

The concept of change, i.e., reinventing myself, came to be, and I had
some great help regarding how to make it a reality.

Memory flashback: In the late 1990s, the new business was in full
swing and I traveled the country to locate executives for universities and
healthcare systems in the western states of the country.

On a business trip from Houston, TX, to San Francisco, I happened
to sit next to the well-known author, John Gray. He wrote the marvelous
best seller, *Men Are from Mars, Women Are from Venus.*

During our four-hour flight, he shared his thoughts on how important
changes were to life, no matter what it took to make those changes, in

order to find a measure of peace and happiness. The concept made sense, and hearing about it from someone who had such an influence on so many people, was a godsend. Of course, we all know there are no coincidences in life and experiences happen for a reason. That's when I decided to write this book.

We continued to talk and as I shared my struggle with losing a son, he suggested that a change in thought and attitude might be something I ought to consider. He used the term "reinventing yourself" as a possibility, which was something he was familiar with. What he said made a great deal of sense and I decided, then and there, that it would be something I did for my life.

Reflection: *Change in one's life is good even though getting to a better place is difficult to accomplish. The journey may seem like a rough and rocky road with hurdles that appear difficult to overcome, but the "end game" is worth it.*

*   *   *

I took John Gray's advice to heart and began to plan for a change in thought and a change in attitude. I threw myself into building a successful company once again and was fortunate to have a number of new accounts that kept me busy and on the road. My self-confidence was high, as was my trust in people. With all the new activity coming so quickly, it was evident that I needed to hire professional help.

I hired a part-time secretary and a part-time accountant. At a finance committee meeting at our church, I met a fellow parishioner who was starting his own accounting practice. Jim also had an office down the hall from me in the same building where I worked, so we agreed to establish a program that would have him take care of my company's accounting needs.

I left town on Monday mornings and returned to the office on Friday afternoons. Jim and I agreed that his new accounting firm could accommodate paying the bills for the company, pay the estimated taxes, and keep track of company expenses. Back then, it seemed logical to me that signing a series of blank checks prior to leaving town on Monday was a safe thing to do. I trusted him, mainly because he was the chairman of the church's finance committee. I took great comfort in knowing that my bills were paid while I was away on business. Business was better than ever, and I was working on the new me and, first and foremost, it called for me to trust people.

What I failed to realize was that trust was one thing, and being a smart businessman who ought to pay attention to the details, was an entirely different matter.

At one point, the bank inadvertently sent me two envelopes of canceled checks instead of sending them to Jim's office. When I scanned the checks, I noticed an inordinate number of checks had been assigned to Jim's company.

He was skimming thousands of dollars from my company, which was problematic, to say the least. But besides that, he wasn't paying my vendors either. Bottom line was, I couldn't dig the company out of the hole we were in and was forced to file Chapter 7 bankruptcy.

That was another blow to the idea that sobriety was a wonderful place to be (ha-ha). This time, however, the responsibility was on my shoulders for not paying attention to the details of running a company with best practices as the driver for success. I wasn't happy about it; I was angry and upset, but I could own my role in what resulted. That gave me a lot of power in a very difficult situation.

Despite the disappointment and betrayal I experienced at a personal level, I still believed sobriety was the correct place to be, and I believed I'd recover in terms of my business, as well.

* * *

As this was occurring, I began my serious studies of *A Course in Miracles*. This new way of viewing the world brought great insight and clarity into my life.

While studying the *Course*, I could, with discipline and through consistently reading the *Workbook for Students*, feel a shift in my perception of my world and the world around me.

A Course in Miracles describes a philosophy based not on what "is" or "is not," but rather on the interconnectedness of body, mind, spirit, and the world. All things are connected yet retain individuality. As I mentioned in my introduction to this book, the *Course* sums it up like this: *"Nothing real can be threatened. Nothing unreal exists. Herein lies the peace of God."*

The *Course* stresses forgiveness, which played a large role in allowing me to move beyond the problems Jim created for me and my company.

Yes, I said forgiveness. Not an easy thing to do when a "friend" has buried your company. To be honest, I haven't *forgotten* Jim's actions, but I have managed to *forgive* him.

I confronted him one-on-one and was even civil when I did it. My attorney counseled me to forego prosecuting him because he had cleverly manufactured and doctored time sheets of his work for my company that justified the checks he wrote to himself. And I didn't have the finances to launch a civil case against him. So, as the old saying goes, "Once burned, twice cautious."

The company I currently run was established with best business practices, and we enjoy great success. It's amazing how well things go for you when you pay attention to the details. (Smile.) It did require starting back at square one, however.

* * *

Many times, it seemed that the deeper I delved into my spiritual journey, the more difficult the lessons in my life became. It was as though I had to experience a series of events in order to purge, or rid myself, of old behaviors before I was able to move forward.

I wondered if life would continue to be nothing more than a series of catastrophic events, or if at some point I would actually manifest some semblance of peace and serenity.

The spiritual development books I read and enjoyed so much pointed toward learning how to bring changes into my existence in the here and now. If I devoted time and energy through meditation, I could accomplish what I wanted in my life.

This concept suggested that if I sat quietly locked into the universe, communicated with God or my Higher Power, and talked to my spirit guides, I could manifest the changes I wanted, for a life filled with peace, serenity, and prosperity.

Since my life had taken so many turns which at the time seemed horribly negative, I decided to stay the course and pursue mightily and consistently, the new endeavor called *daily meditation*. After all, why not pursue it? Everything else I was doing seemed to abort the results I sought.

Not coincidentally, thwarted intentions and lack of peace were especially evident whenever I thought I was in control and that I was "the one driving the bus," so to speak.

*   *   *

Learning how to meditate was not easy because I wasn't very disciplined about finding quiet time each day or in training myself with a specific method or type of practice.

Now the Internet is filled with great information relative to meditation and the various methods that others have explored and developed successfully. But my pursuit to gain credible knowledge regarding meditation really came into focus when a friend suggested that I check out a place in Wisconsin called The Christine Center for Meditation. The Center is located forty miles south of Eau Claire, Wisconsin, in the heart of dairy and farm country.

The Center is like an oasis in the desert. Established in 1980 by two Franciscan Sisters from Wheaton, Illinois, it provides both modern and rustic accommodations for all who visit there.

The core group of nuns who maintain the Center are highly trained in methods of meditation, holistic organic food, and virtually all spiritual matters. I attended the Center on weekends and began to immerse myself in programs that brought training and insight relative to the methods of meditation. The Center also offers a wide range of programs, and is truly life-giving for those travelers who seek a new and better way to journey through this world.

The method of meditation I learned at the Center is still a part of my daily routine, although I have added new practices from time to time. I had to overcome several of the major hurdles that all practitioners face, namely: finding quiet time each day, sitting or kneeling in a comfortable place, clearing my mind of the facts, figures, worries, and other things we have in our lives that seem to drive us to distraction.

Once I did that, my meditations were deeper and more complete. Overcoming each of those "bumps in the process" put me on the road to experience greater insight as to who I was and what I needed to do to change.

* * *

The experience at Hazelden taught me valuable lessons along with insights into how people behave when confronted with the vicissitudes of life.

For those of us who have a propensity toward alcoholism or other addictions, behaviors are often manifested in strange and unpleasant ways.

Certainly at the core of my behavior was the fact that I had inherited the gene for alcoholism. Another core aspect was how I dealt with stress and the trauma of losing a child. I'd learned those coping mechanisms from the family dynamics I was raised with. Those family patterns, in a sense, dictated how I would act things out.

People often say that we tend to parent and raise our children the way we were parented *as* children. I believe that to be true, unless we make a stern and forceful attempt to do things differently from the way we were raised. Of course, we have to be aware that how we were raised is impacting how we behave as adults.

When I shared my family history with the core group at Hazelden, I told a story that related to a family incident I could never figure out.

I mentioned to the group that I'd often heard my mother whisper to other adults in the house, "Don't tell little Henry."

Well, since my dad was big Henry, I guessed that meant they were referring to me as "little Henry." Our group counselor explained that it was typical for an alcoholic family to have "secrets." Unfortunately for me, I never found out what those secrets were all about and why there was such a need to keep information from me. It bothered me for years and I always felt like an outsider in my own family.

I'd been at Hazelden about two weeks into the twenty-eight-day program when I learned one of the most important bits of information I would learn from those core group meetings.

The counselor led the discussion that day and spent an entire afternoon explaining the work of a psychiatrist by the name of Dr. Albert Ellis. From the Dr. Albert Ellis's website, his theory is explained as follows:

> *Albert Ellis, Ph.D., was a clinical psychologist who trained as a psychoanalyst. Early in his career, he became disillusioned with the slow progress of his clients. He noticed that they got better much quicker once they changed their ways of thinking about themselves and their problems. In 1955 he developed Rational Emotive Behavior Therapy (REBT). Rational Emotive Behavior Therapy (REBT) is now a widely practiced, comprehensive, and highly effective form of psychotherapy. In addition to being a proven therapy, REBT offers an approach to life that leads to greater fulfillment and happiness. At the heart of REBT are the concepts of unconditional self-acceptance, unconditional other-acceptance, and unconditional life-acceptance.*

The concept made sense to me even though, at the time, I didn't fully comprehend what it meant. But it gave me a place to start and I began to read Dr. Ellis's research.

To change how we *think* about a situation or a person can, and will, alter how we *feel* about them. We are feeling beings, and so we react to people and situations with emotion.

To learn that I could choose to see things in a different light was an awakening for me. A prime example had to do with how and where I grew up.

We lived in a tough neighborhood in New York City, which dictated to a large degree how I related and reacted to those around me. As a teenager, for instance, if someone voiced an opinion toward me that I took as threatening or just didn't like, my adopted automatic response was one of quick anger laced with several choice expletives for special effect. (Enter the purposeful and mighty effective use of the "f—" word.)

I learned that an angry, disrespectful, and tough-guy response wasn't always necessary. Rather, I understood, or at least I thought I understood, that the individual who spoke those things might have been hurting emotionally for reasons that had nothing to do with me.

And if I caused someone else to be upset, then it was my responsibility to right the wrong that was committed and handle it in a peaceful manner.

A Course in Miracles proposes that we, in times of verbal attack from someone, reach out to them in a loving way and assist them as they work through whatever it is that is upsetting them. That in itself is not always an easy thing to do. However, I found that the more centered and the more secure I was with myself, the easier it was to respond in a loving, peaceful manner.

Once we get it and practice it, it's miraculous to witness how the entire dynamic changes in a heartbeat. Perception. It all boils down to perception—how you see the world and how you respond to situations and the people you interact with.

I have firsthand experience that this works because when I attend places filled with holy, prayerful people, or stay at a meditation center, for example, the folks attending these places are generally at peace with themselves and are able to respond to others accordingly, regardless of the dynamics involved.

* * *

I mentioned earlier that prior to leaving the Mayo Clinic we were told that 85 percent of the couples who lose a child will divorce. And, as I said, Grace and I talked about it and both decided that marriage counseling would be the next logical step for us.

However, after two and a half years it became evident that we were not going to be able to make our marriage work. Over the years, I've reflected on why our marriage didn't survive.

Two issues seem to make the most sense to me. When two people experience a traumatic event simultaneously in their lives, each deals with that experience in his and her own way.

In our case, we lost a child and the pain and anguish was so deep and so profound that each of us could only take care of the hurt that we had inside. All the while, we couldn't understand why our mate couldn't "save" us from the interminable pain. It became a lose-lose situation rather quickly, and it was only a matter of time before our relationship began to unravel.

My wife dealt with her pain and sorrow in her own way. And even though I tried, I was unable, and at times unwilling, to give her the emotional support she needed. Her emotional needs became overwhelming for me.

We both hurt deeply and neither of us could help the other while each of us was trying to survive.

That's only one aspect of our failed relationship, however. Another issue was how we began to heal ourselves. In time, we started to move and grow in different directions. Each of us wanted to be something more than we were before all hell broke loose. In addition to the loss of Dan and my struggling marriage, I was dealing with my alcoholic behavior and the pain I'd caused family and friends that I loved.

Obviously, not everyone grows at the same rate, nor do they necessarily grow in the same direction. Therein lies the basis of discontent and angst.

Grace and I finally came to the point where we decided that we needed to step away from the relationship and make a break of it if we were to find any measure of peace and happiness in our lives.

The good news was that we're now very willing and able to help each other as we continue to stay involved with our family. Major change in our lives started with a separation.

*   *   *

Our separation, although difficult, had some redeeming value, to say the least. I needed space to think and collect my thoughts. Where was my life headed? Where was I headed?

With my consulting company slowly growing again, I had steady financial income and was responsible enough to offer my wife assistance with the basic bills, but I certainly didn't have much more.

I began to live life with less. Before that time, spending money was something I never paid much attention to, as it was almost always self-centered and self-indulgent.

Simplicity has merits. When I moved away from the relationship with my wife and the house, I rented a room on the top floor of a Franciscan retreat center called the Tao Center, in the same town I lived in. It was a quiet time for the Center since it was "off season" for the usual number of people who sought retreats. I was sequestered on the third floor of one of the empty wings of the building.

The irony here, since again a group of Catholic (Franciscan) Sisters came to my aid, was not lost on me. The Catholic Church, which had so disillusioned me, has always been in my life to help me pick up the pieces and put myself back together.

Remember that I said there are no coincidences and that things do happen for a reason? I suspect the fact that Saint Francis has always been a hero of mine had something to do with where I ended up as I began the next chapter in my life.

Even though my nights were peaceful, they were lonely and I doubted myself, constantly wondering if I'd made the right decision to move away from my family. I found it amusing that I missed some things that I'd never paid a whole lot of attention to. Things like mowing the lawn and taking the dogs for long walks. It was easy to feel sorry for myself, even though I was the one who'd brought all of this into my life.

Then our divorce was finalized. For anyone who's been through a divorce, my heart goes out to you. It's demeaning and hurtful for everyone involved. It screams to everyone that you have failed (by this point we all know how I hate to fail). And like it or not, attorneys get involved and things can get ugly. Much angst and sorrow prevailed for both of us and our three surviving sons.

There's a song by The Rolling Stones, titled "You Can't Always Get What You Want." I'm not sure if it was meant to be prophetic or not, but the words ring true for many people who are on a spiritual journey and have an awareness of the challenges they experience. A portion of the lyrics are: ". . . you can't always get what you want / But if you try sometime, you just might find / You get what you need . . ." Ah, yes. How true that is!

How many times have we joked about the fact that we'd better watch out what we're wishing for because we might get it? Of course, at the time when things happen we tend to judge them as either good or bad. Sometimes even though experiences seem to be negative, like when your accountant embezzles money from your company, after time has passed, the experience proves to be the best thing that could have happened. Hindsight is indeed 20/20.

The Franciscan Retreat Center, or The Tao Center, was a marvelous experience and the beginning of my spiritual quest to find answers about myself.

*   *   *

Step 4 of the Twelve Step Program states: "Made a searching and fearless moral inventory of ourselves."

People in recovery in the Twelve Step Program are encouraged to take an honest personal inventory of their past experiences and behaviors. I did that at Hazelden, but it became apparent it was time to do it again. A.A. encourages people to do this inventory with another person in the program, especially if that person has several years of sobriety in their lives.

I took inventory to assess where I'd been over the past several years and what that might tell me about who I was at that point in my life. It required that I look at my self-deceptions, my flaws, and the fears that I still harbored. All pretty scary stuff, actually, because at forty-six years of age, I'd been through a whole heap of difficult experiences, and I really didn't want to look at it further even though I knew it was the best thing to do.

Of course, I did realize that most of what I'd experienced was my own doing, so it was time to dig deep and be totally honest with myself.

As it states in *The Twelve Steps and Twelve Traditions* book of A.A., Step 4 is our vigorous and painstaking effort to discover what the liabilities in each of us have been, and are. We want to find exactly how, when, and where our natural desires have warped us. We wish to look squarely at the unhappiness this has caused others and ourselves. By discovering what our emotional deformities are, we can move toward their correction.

Without a willing and persistent effort to do this, there can be little sobriety or contentment for us. Without a searching and fearless moral inventory, most of us have found that the faith which really works in daily living is still out of reach.

As I reviewed my life up to that point, my inventory revealed the following:

- Experienced a divorce from my wife of twenty-five years.
- Lost a business because I didn't pay attention to details and totally misunderstood the meaning of trust. Blind trust in people does not and should not supersede the "best practices" of running a company.
- Went through the Twelve Step Program at Hazelden Treatment Center in Center City, Minnesota. A positive sign and change in my life. A new beginning.
- Survived the death of a son, just barely. Was drinking to excess and constantly fighting to control a vicious anger which eventually morphed into a severe faith crisis.

The goal was to be fearless in reviewing my past experiences, but I also needed to gain some understanding about how things happened and why they happened the way they did.

From that point forward, I imagined I could piece together the answers which would lead me to a plan of complete recovery with some direction for my future. Undoing the hurt that I'd caused many people was also part and parcel of the plan.

I also hoped for the blessing of forgiveness from those I'd hurt and an opportunity to pass on some measure of wisdom I had gained from my past experiences.

Going through the fourth step again was a turning point for me. It was a giant step in my spiritual growth and my return to a belief that God was a loving God and not a dastardly spirit that destroyed people's lives.

If I've said it once, I've said it a thousand times—it was the Twelve Step Program that brought me back from the brink of throwing all religion out of my life.

*   *   *

During my time at the Franciscan Retreat Center I formulated how I was going to change things in my life. Although I didn't realize it then, I was building a program which inevitably culminated in my reinvention.

Several months into my time living there, I was out jogging one Saturday afternoon when I met an old friend of mine, Don. He said he was chasing his dream of starting a business in, of all places, Hawaii. He needed someone to live in his house and wanted to know if I was willing.

Yikes, what a deal! His house overlooked the Mississippi River, high on a bluff across the Minnesota border, in the bucolic hills of western Wisconsin. The area surrounding the house was ideal: private, with fantastic views of the river and the bluffs of Minnesota.

I stayed there for two years. I continued to work as a consultant, and it became clear that I was barely earning enough to sustain myself and my ex-wife. It was obviously time for me to look for a "real" job. I forged ahead and learned some valuable lessons during my time there. I learned how to live with less. I baked my own bread and learned to cook for myself. Can't say my meals ranked right up there with the gourmet chefs, but I survived.

Shortly after I settled into "the house on the bluffs," the IRS came calling and wanted to know how I was going to pay all those back taxes that I owed from the failed business.

I didn't realize it then, but the accountant had also failed to send the estimated tax payments along with the large checks he was writing to himself. Again, I had to face the consequences of not paying attention to the business, but I could choose to give myself yet another emotional beating, or concede that what was done was done. I obtained information on how to deal with the IRS. I learned that in some cases, a reasonable plan could be negotiated. I was told that how successful I'd be in the negotiation really depended on the agent assigned to work with me. I prayed I'd have an agent with a sympathetic soul.

I had a very reasonable-minded agent and negotiated a fair settlement. And I settled my bill. The faith in my Higher Power began to strengthen as I learned how to handle life's challenges more peacefully.

I kept reassuring myself that my lot in life would change if only I would believe it would. I knew I had to find a discipline that would bring good things into my life. I began working in a much more dedicated way to bring about a spiritual renewal.

Enter *A Course in Miracles* full-time and on a consistent basis. It was the first step of several that put me on the path of spiritual growth and finding a system that would help me transform my life.

I began with a daily reading from the *Workbook for Students*. In time, I had read and understood the 365 lessons that outlined a way to change how I viewed the world. I slowly transformed my thought process, which allowed me to see how significant my ego had been in directing my thoughts and actions. As is the case with most human beings, my ego had dictated my actions and reactions throughout my life. My ego still serves as a powerful part of my psyche, but today I understand the force behind it and can work with it and understand how it keeps driving to be in control and "rule my thoughts."

Now I catch myself when ego-thoughts occur that have in the past caused upset or hurtful things to happen. I can pull back and tell myself, "Whoa, buddy, you don't want to go there."

And, to be honest, it works *most* of the time; after all, I'm a work in progress. *A Course in Miracles* made a lot of sense to me, and in a matter of days I began to see a shift in my perception of the world in which I functioned.

On day five, for instance, the lesson read: "I am never upset for the reason I think."

On day six, the reading was: "I am upset because I see something that is not there."

And, on day seven, the reading was: "I only see the past."

I slowly increased my awareness of how I perceived the world, and I allowed myself to see it as it truly was, without my ego telling me how *it* perceived the world. That lesson and control has made a profound difference in my life.

Chapter Nine

Dreams

"Your only obligation in any lifetime is to be true to yourself.
Being true to anyone else or anything else is . . . impossible.
—Richard Bach, *Illusions: The Adventures of a Reluctant Messiah*

I continued to stay disciplined with the *Course*, and set several goals for my future. Aside from the spiritual work I was involved in, I wanted to learn how to sail, and to travel to new places. But beyond that, I wanted my own sailboat.

On a Sunday afternoon in mid-February, as I gazed out of the large picture window that made up one entire wall of the bluff house, I looked down at the frozen Mississippi River. It was minus twenty degrees Fahrenheit, but I was snuggled in a warm, cozy A-frame house heated by a big Franklin wood-burning stove.

I said to myself that day, "I want to sail around the world."

Several problems arose *immediately* with that declaration. I was in a deep financial hole. I didn't own a boat and couldn't afford to buy one. On top of that, I lived in or near the Land of 10,000 Lakes, yet far from any ocean. But hey, why not dream to the max?

As I've mentioned many times in the past, if we don't dream the dream, we won't have the reality. We need to start with the dream.

* * *

Reflection: *I totally embrace the idea of living my life as though it were my own and to heck with what others say or think. It takes great courage to be the person we want to be.*

A couple of sailing friends who owned sailboats on Lake Pepin, Wisconsin, near where I lived, spoke often of sailing to the Bahamas and reveled in the mystery of crossing the Gulf Stream on the way to islands of paradise in the Caribbean.

Even though John Gray's book, *How to Get What You Want and Want What You Have,* wasn't written yet, in it he states: "The secret to personal success is to be true to yourself and to continue to want more. To achieve personal success, it is not enough to be happy. You must also grow in your desire for more. Passion is power. When you really want more, you will get it."

I lived the reality of those words and didn't care what others thought about my dream, even though several people criticized me for it. I was told once by a friend, that my dream of sailing around the world was simply my way of escaping reality, and my friend wanted to know what I was running from.

Rubbish! I figured it was my life and my dream. It was all I had at the time and I was holding on to it.

One day I was reading the Minneapolis Sunday newspaper and saw an ad for sailing lessons on Lake Superior. The captain, a fellow named Carl, from Minneapolis, listed the program as one that included discussions about *A Course in Miracles* and included sailing on the lake in a forty-foot Tartan. I thought that was pretty clever, so I signed up to be a part of the program.

It was everything I'd hoped. I learned how to sail and gained a new perspective on the teachings of the *Course.* Upon my completion of the sailing lessons Carl told me to go buy myself a fourteen- to sixteen-foot day-sailing boat and *really* learn how to sail.

His thought was that once you trimmed and set the sails on a big boat, it basically sailed itself. But not so in a small boat, because the shifting winds moved the smaller boat out of trim quickly, meaning I'd have to pay attention and make sail trim changes constantly.

I followed his instructions and eventually owned a small boat on Lake Pepin. That proved to be the beginning of an important step in building an incredible relationship with my current wife.

*   *   *

At that same time I was an avid reader of *Wooden Boat* magazine and fell in love with the whole idea of wooden boats. The natural feel, the texture, and the smell of wood seemed so clean and pure in comparison to boats made of fiberglass. And the thought that a once living organism was now transformed into a classically designed sailing vessel was, in itself, appealing as well.

Perhaps there was some connection to the notion of the blade of grass idea and my son Daniel's response to the sermon given by Father John five or six years prior. At any rate, I pushed the envelope of my dream to have a sailboat, and in one of the issues of the magazine, I read an article about a fellow out in Martha's Vineyard who'd restored a 1929 John Alden designed schooner called the Malabar II. I had already become a fan of John Alden sailboats, and found the photo in the magazine of the Malabar II under sail electrifying.

I did what any sensible wooden boat enthusiast would do; I telephoned him and asked if I might come for a visit to see the newly restored Malabar II. I shared with him my keen interest in the Malabar series of sailboats.

His response was a resounding, "Absolutely, come on over and take a look at her."

So, on a business trip to NYC the next spring, I made arrangements to see the boat. Even better, I was given a fantastic sail on her. I cherish that memory to this day.

I was really smitten with wooden boats, to say the least, so I contacted the John Alden Foundation and was able to purchase a set of lofting plans and drawings for a forty-three-foot schooner similar to the Malabar II. Back home and living in the hills of western Wisconsin, I was surrounded by a variety of hardwood trees.

Another friend of mine lived on ten acres of forested land and had a great stand of white oaks. I bartered with him, and we field-cut five white oak trees into rough-cut beams and frames, and stacked it in my big driveway. I had enough timber to build the Malabar II.

While I thought that was a sure sign I was on my way to fulfilling my dream of owning a wooden sailboat, the boat was not a reality at that time. I had many more lessons to experience before a sailboat showed up in my life.

*　　*　　*

In his book, *The Monk Who Sold His Ferrari,* Robin Sharma writes of a statement that Julian makes to his colleague, John, one of the protagonists in the book.

> *Enthusiasm is one of the key ingredients for a lifetime of successful living, and I am glad that you still have every ounce of yours. Earlier I taught you that we each think about 60,000 thoughts on an average day. By writing out your desires and goals on a piece of paper, you send a red flag to your subconscious mind that these thoughts are far more important than the remaining 59,999 other ones. Your mind will then start to seek out all opportunities to realize your destiny like a guided missile. It is really a very scientific process. Most of us are simply not aware of it.*

Reflection: *It's great to plan for our future and set our dreams down on paper. I truly believe there is power in that exercise. The step in the process that we fail to consider initially, sometimes, is that we don't understand our starting point in the process. In other words: I clearly had the horse in front of the cart in that I manifested the wood for the boat, but I didn't express my deep desire (with passion) that I wanted to manifest the sailboat and not just the wood.*

*　　*　　*

Working as a consultant, I was on a business trip in Milwaukee, Wisconsin, and one evening, stopped in to browse through a Barnes & Noble bookstore. Something happened that has occurred several times throughout my life. A book—a pamphlet, actually—fell off the bookshelf and landed near my feet. Not thinking, I bent over and picked it up to put it back on the shelf. Before replacing it, I began to page through the book. As fate would have it, it was the first book written by Louise L. Hay, and it was, I believe, the precursor to her now very successful and famous book, *You Can Heal Your Life.*

I bought the little book and was intrigued by what she had to say about how we can create a life of health and happiness by changing how we think. She advocated that we can take charge of our lives and our health by understanding the root cause of the disease that we experience. It all sounded very familiar to me, and I flashed back to the message from Dr. Albert Ellis.

Other authors suggested also, that if we'd identify the cause of our pain, we can, with an appropriate affirmation, heal ourselves.

I determined what I needed to correct, or change, in my life and matched up the correct affirmation. While some people call these positive thoughts "affirmations" and others call them "mantras," it doesn't really matter. It's the discipline and the daily work that matters. I started saying my affirmations every day.

I kept at it when I was involved in seemingly mindless activities, like jogging, painting the house, or mowing the lawn. I have to admit it was humbling when it dawned on me that I had an awful lot of work to do to rid myself of some pesky demons.

But I was committed to living a healthy, powerful, and joy-filled life, so I was willing to go with the flow and try to make it work. Now, many "experts" write that it's impossible for us to completely erase all those old "childhood" tapes that run in our subconscious—the ones that remind us our parents told us we were stupid, or fat, or slow, or ugly, or whatever. Or the memories of the times we learned that crying in public could get us beat up, or that not being chosen for stickball meant we were losers.

All of those types of experiences, from the early years to the young adult years, have an effect on our psyche. So here we are now, a grown-up, an adult trying to erase those hurtful messages. We can't do it. But there is hope.

You can, with diligent, consistent hard work, minimize the power of those memories by replacing them with new, positive, and truthful affirmations. That's one of the powerful messages that Louise Hay stamped solidly on my mind. Replace, replace, replace! I began to play my new "tapes" over and over in my mind, especially when I went jogging.

* * *

In the summer months in Minnesota, running and jogging around the lakes was the thing to do. Two friends, both runners, made life bearable for me by urging me to run every day.

John, a salesman at a local furniture store, and Andy, the executive director of the local YMCA, were two inspiring guys. Running every day was great therapy for me, and I'll never forget how they stayed with me and pushed me to run when I was struggling with so much anger.

It's because of their unselfish behavior and great example that I find it easy to help others. There is a proactive movie titled *Pay It Forward*, with actors Kevin Spacey and Helen Hunt. The theme of the movie is that you do an act of kindness for someone without wanting or expecting anything in return. You simply say to the person on the receiving end, here's a gift for you. Just pass it on and do something kind for someone who is not expecting anything in return. What a great concept.

Reflection: *The kindness shown to me from John and Andy has meant so much to me in my recovery. Remember to give back to people, pay it forward, and watch it be a transformative act for the entire world to see.*

* * *

Running many miles each day was cathartic. Slowly the anger that I held on to for so long started to dissipate.

At the time, though I logged fifty to sixty miles a week, I didn't think of running in marathon races. In actuality, I was building a strong base to do just that. Our little YMCA had a group of eighteen to twenty runners and all decided to run in marathons. I decided to join them. At 185 pounds,

I was way too heavy for a marathon runner. I ran and trained with guys who were lighter and younger.

My first goal was to finish a marathon, *period*. My second goal was to do it somewhere near the three-hour mark. My first time was three hours and sixteen minutes, or roughly a little over a seven-minute-per-mile pace for the 26.2 miles.

The significance of that experience is that it launched me toward a time of great confidence in myself. So much so, that I took to running religiously.

*   *   *

The success in running as a forty-year-old pushed aside many self-doubts, and I encourage others who are in need of a confidence builder to find something similar. It's a major first step in achieving bigger goals.

For me, it was a means to prove to myself that my athleticism was still valid, which has always been meaningful to me. But even more important, it was proof that I could set a goal and achieve it, no matter how lofty it seemed at the time.

Over the course of a mere three years prior to my first marathon, I'd lost a son, gone through treatment for alcoholism, experienced a failed business, tackled the IRS, and survived a divorce. My psyche was hammered, and it was important to find a way to do *more* than survive.

I wanted to be healthy, both psychologically and physically. While running took care of me physically, *A Course in Miracles* and Louise Hay's "little blue book" of affirmations took care of my psyche.

Running outside each day continued, but the winter months in Minnesota and Wisconsin drove most runners indoors. And so I headed for the indoor track at the YMCA for my workouts. I came up with a new plan to see if I could really quicken the healing process for my psyche by following a disciplined regimen using several affirmations. I chose several Louise Hay affirmations that fit my purposes and began to experience change.

Since I'd lived through the embarrassment of losing a business, I thought it appropriate to begin with "I am worthy of success," which I still use today. And, since I'd experienced a failed marriage, I chose "I am worthy of a loving relationship."

The indoor track at the YMCA had twenty-five laps to the mile and I was intent on running five miles a day. That made 125 laps per workout. With each lap around the track, I could repeat one of the affirmations approximately thirty times per lap. With thirty affirmations multiplied by twenty-five laps, that came to 750 affirmations per mile. When I ran the 125 laps and multiplied it by thirty affirmations, I had repeated them approximately 3,750 times.

Now, before you decide that I'm totally whacked, I didn't do that *every* day, but I was committed to making a drastic change in my thinking so I could change how I felt about myself and what was going on in my life.

* * *

In her book, *You Can Heal Your Life*, Louise L. Hay writes: "Cleaning the mental house after a lifetime of indulging in negative mental thoughts is a bit like going on a good nutritional program after years of indulging in junk foods. They both can often create healing crises. As you begin to change your physical diet, the body begins to throw off the accumulation of toxic residue, and as this happens, you can feel rather rotten for a day or two. So it is when you make a decision to the mental thought patterns—your circumstances can begin to seem worse for a while."

She continues with: "It's the same with cleaning up dried-on crusty mental patterns. When we soak it with new ideas, all the gook comes to the surface to look at. Just keep doing the affirmations, and soon you will have totally cleared an old limitation."

Reflection: *Keep on keeping on even when it seems futile and a pain in the butt to do all the inner work "stuff." If we're going to change, we have to continue to find a system that will work for each of us.*

* * *

An important thing for me to overcome was "living in a fishbowl." The town of Winona had a population of 20,000 souls and everyone knew everyone else's business.

I was faced with seeing a lot of familiar people around town all the time, and I needed to make some corrections, or else continue to live with shame and embarrassment. I didn't plan to explore the aspect of shame in my recovery, but it became apparent that I had to deal with it.

I discussed the aspect of shame with several people in the A.A. program who were also in recovery. I was told that shame was a significant factor and roadblock in the recovery process. So, once again, I was faced with another hurdle. I had to move through and beyond not only guilt and self-doubt, but also *shame*.

In her article titled "Shame," Jan Luckingham Fable writes:

> *At times shame and guilt are used interchangeably, but they are not the same at all—although it isn't unusual for both to exist simultaneously. Guilt is more concerned with doing something, with transgressions, while shame is about a perceived failure of being, being unworthy, unwanted or bad. Guilty people fear punishment. Shamed people fear abandonment. Shame is not all bad, though. It can have great value if we are not overwhelmed by it. There would be no sense of privacy or intimacy without shame. Because shame is an uncomfortable feeling, a person who is not overwhelmed by it can use it to alter his or her behavior. Healthy shame tells us something is wrong in our lives and motivates us to change. Healthy shame is temporary. Excessive shame is not.*

Reflection: *Shame played a major role in driving me forward to engage in a program of reinventing myself, and this exercise was an important first step in opening myself to a new awareness of self-help.*

* * *

On another note, self-doubt is something that most people deal with on a daily basis. I have found that at times it can be limiting and debilitating. However, it can also be a great teacher and something that propels us forward to succeed, since we must face it square-on if we're going to succeed.

I put self-doubt right up there with fear of failure. I once heard a marketing executive say, "I'm not sure if I am a success because I truly want to succeed or because I'm so afraid of failing." I've had many moments of self-doubt involving all manner of circumstances. At times, it was detrimental to achieve the goals I had set for myself. However, there have also been instances when I had to "bull my neck," so to speak, to gain the outcome that I sought.

For example, once, when I was about forty-eight years old, I served as a novice crew member on a forty-foot sloop with two seasoned sailors, both of whom had previously circumnavigated the globe.

The trip began in Bermuda, destination Fort Lauderdale, Florida, to deliver the captain's boat for resale. It was my turn at the helm and I was "on watch" for the next four hours. I started my watch at midnight in seas that were like being on a roller coaster. As the other two slept below, I was left to handle the boat.

Long about two o'clock in the morning, I was tired, hungry, and cold and wet from the spray which came over the port gunnels. The night was pitch-black and I couldn't see anything beyond the bow of the boat. I got spooked. I had never been across the ocean prior to this, and the boat was surfing down big swells.

My mind started to wander, and I wondered what I would do if we ran into something, like a semi-submerged container that had slipped overboard from one of those big oceangoing container ships. I'd been told it happened often. I started to doubt that I could really do what I was charged to do, sail the boat.

I heard myself say, "I can't do this," and I wanted to quit. Again I heard myself say, "Then why the hell are you out here, anyway? You must be stupid or something."

Then another voice said, "Oh, shut the hell up and steer the boat. After all, this is what you wanted to do. You wanted to learn how to sail on the ocean."

The internal "argument" kept up for the next several hours, until I finally declared that I was indeed capable and was going to be a good sailor someday, so just shut up and pay the dues!

When my shift ended, I headed below for some incredibly sound sleep.

Before I drifted off to sleep, though, I recollected some advice given to me by Brother Raymond, from Saint Mary's University.

"Henry, remember that adversity introduces a man to himself."

I agree with Brother Ray and I would add that adversity also offers a person a choice of options to look at, self-doubt being one of them. We have to make a choice to rise above that doubt, to find success.

*   *   *

I read an article on the Web which mentioned that Dr. Kenneth Wapnick and his wife, Gloria, were open to putting on *Course* seminars and workshops across the country.

Dr. Kenneth Wapnick is a clinical psychologist and his association with the *Course* dates back to 1972, when he met Helen Schucman and William Thetford in New York City, shortly after the scribing of the *Course* was completed there. He worked closely with Helen in editorially organizing the *Course* manuscript and preparing it for publication.

Gloria Wapnick was a social studies teacher and dean of students in a Bronx (New York) high school. Her work with the *Course* began in 1977, when she started a group to study and discuss the *Course's* teachings.

I called them and asked if they would come to Minnesota to host a workshop. They readily agreed and put on a marvelous program. It's one thing to study a program from books or tapes, but to meet two people who virtually were living proof that the principles and message of the *Course* actually can work, was an incredible inspiration to all of us in the seminar.

Reflection: *Blessings abound when we're fortunate to be in the presence of, and can talk with, an individual who personifies peace and unconditional love. Seek them out—we are better for having done so.*

Whenever I talked to Ken, I felt I was in the presence of an enlightened being and someone who had the authentic experience and knowledge to teach how *A Course in Miracles* could be manifested in one's life.

For example, one day Ken and I were walking toward each other to say hello.

As he came closer, I said, "Hey Ken, how are you?" Then I blurted out, "You know, Ken, your white shirt with the blue stripes makes you look like a referee."

And without missing a beat he said, "Hey, what did I ever do to you that you would make fun of my shirt?"

I thought for a moment and my retort was defensive when I said, "I'm really not making fun of your shirt, I didn't mean it that way."

His response was, "Ah, but you did, or else you wouldn't have thought it and you wouldn't have said it, so you decided to judge my shirt as something other than the nice shirt that it is. But that's okay, I forgive you and I know that you were trying to be funny at my expense."

That was an exchange I hadn't planned on. It was, however, something I'll never forget. I saw what I wanted to see instead of seeing what was there. I was confronted by my own lack of confidence and decided to project those feelings onto Ken by poking fun at his shirt. In reality, his shirt didn't look anything like a referee's shirt.

I've reflected on that simple communication many times and realize that it's easy and mindless to judge others. It seems when I try to be funny or make a joke it will most often come at someone else's expense. Or, I busy myself with judging them somehow inferior to me. Instead of accepting others for who they are, I'm quick to say to myself, *Wow, look at how fat or skinny that person is,* or *Gee, look at those silly tattoos.*

The good news is, when you don't judge other people, it's actually freeing to let people be who they are. In doing so, I don't go to that place where I need to take someone else's inventory. It is what it is and they are who they are, so let people be who they are without judging them.

I was determined to do what was needed to make significant changes in my life. Obviously, an awful lot of work went into my program of self-help so that I could gain a new awareness of who I really was and who I wanted to be. I would, from time to time, change the affirmations.

Sometimes I switched to: "I am worthy of abundance," or "I am worthy of a healthy, loving relationship." These exercises, plus my daily work with *A Course in Miracles*, went on for several years.

I continued to spend most weekends at The Christine Center for Meditation. Frequenting the Center turned out to be another powerful step toward gaining valuable insight into the world of my personal spirituality. The beauty of the meditation center, or *ashram*, as it is also called, was twofold:

First – The Center is surrounded by hardwoods and birch trees, with an occasional meadow around the periphery of the 360 acres of farmland owned by the Franciscan Sisters. It's quiet and very peaceful.

Second – There was always a group of people who were on a spiritual quest to find truth and meaning in their lives.

The core group of eight or nine Center teachers lived a simple lifestyle. I was told that originally the group adopted a lifestyle similar to the Israeli religious sect called the Essenes.

The Essenes, by practice and belief, were advanced as a social culture as well as a spiritual group in that they believed in the equality between men and women. Their food was organic and simple, not uncommon for those who lived in that kind of spiritual environment.

All who came to the Center could, if they chose to do so, live that same way. The food served was organic, with little or no red meat or pork, including the poultry which came from the Amish community that lived and farmed in the adjacent area.

*   *   *

Once, when I was walking from my little cabin in the woods, on the way to the meditation loft prior to sunup, a magical scene played out before me. The day hadn't yet received its first kiss of sunshine heralding the start of another day. I walked through large stands of birch, maple, and oak trees as each cast its shadow in the morning mist. Up ahead and off to one side of the path, I saw a large old tree stump that at first gave me a start because it resembled a black bear, which were reputed to roam that area of the woods.

But, not surprisingly, I made it to the loft unscathed and ready to do battle with my psyche through a rigorous meditation practice. I chuckled afterward. Is it tougher to do battle with bears or with one's own psyche?

My daily routine began at 6:30 a.m. with light stretching exercises and Tai Chi movements. This was followed by an hour of silent group meditation, all before breakfast.

One of the great things about being in the meditation center was that I was surrounded by other seekers and practitioners all the time, so it was easier to stay at it with others who were doing the same thing. The meditation group generally had ten to twelve participants who sat or knelt in a quiet, prayerful atmosphere.

After an hour or so, the facilitator hit the ceramic bowl and with a clang that sounded like something heard in a Chinese monastery, the session ended. Slowly we came back to our senses and reentered the "real" world. Moving out of the converted hayloft, we went downstairs to have a light breakfast.

Breakfast was followed by a lively discussion and/or teaching from one of the core group members. Before lunch we came together as a group for more meditation.

The Center was located on an old farm, so there was always much to do in the way of wholesome work. The afternoon work usually included splitting, stacking, and delivering wood to the hermitages where most of us stayed while attending the Center. It always reminded me of another good book on the subject of meditation, *Chop Wood, Carry water; A Guide to Finding Spiritual Fulfillment in Everyday Life,* by Rick Fields.

As dinnertime approached we participated in another short meditation session. After dinner we shared ideas about meditation techniques or personal philosophies, and then made our way back to the large loft for meditation and evening prayers.

The late-night Compline, or evening prayers, the last prayers of the day, were fashioned after the style of prayer the ancient desert fathers used when monastic life was first developed. Oftentimes, the late meditation involved a group of attendees who participated in a creative visualization practice. At first, I wasn't so sure it was worthwhile as we sat quietly in chairs that had been placed in a circle. The facilitator then dimmed the lights and we were asked to "quiet our minds" in preparation for the session.

After ten minutes passed, the facilitator led us by asking individuals to share what they were seeing or hearing. Mind you, it was very, very quiet, and I was amazed to hear about the images that people shared with us. Some people said they could see the same images that others saw. It was a peaceful, humbling, and enlightening experience.

* * *

Early training in the various meditation techniques taught me that it works best to start the meditation routine by sitting comfortably with the back straight and breathing in a controlled, easy manner. The key is to think about and feel your breath as it crosses your nostrils during the inhale and exhale. It all seemed silly at first. After all, how hard can it be to breathe? But in reality, I found it difficult to concentrate as my mind continued to wander to other things, no matter how mundane they were. I was surprised to learn that effective meditation required considerable discipline and practice.

Chapter Ten

Miracles Begin

There are no accidents in salvation. Those who are to meet will meet,
because together they have the potential for a holy relationship.
They are ready for each other.
From *A Course in Miracles*

Everything happens for a reason, even though we may not think that to be true. At any given moment, something is taking place that will have an effect on our lives.

There was a time when I truly believed that my son's death was the worst thing I could ever experience. I don't believe that now, as I have witnessed, time and again, how incredibly blessed I am. I've grown and our family has changed in so many miraculous ways. Because of my experiences, the measures go far beyond whatever I could have imagined. The depth and meaning of forgiveness and the love that I feel now for myself and toward others, are, in fact, miracles enough.

It's a blessing that we are not in charge. We simply don't have all the information about people, events, places, causes, and the future, to be in charge—there is far too much going on all around the universe for us to even conceive, let alone understand or control. Ever looked back on an event and thought, "Gee, I'm glad such and such did happen, or else I wouldn't have what I have now"? Then you know what I mean.

I think it's best not to take life's trials and tribulations personally, because it all comes back to there being a reason for things to happen. I've also learned that journeying through life with a sense of humor is critical to finding some measure of peace.

*   *   *

Miracles have always come in sequence in my life and I have been privileged to be the recipient of many. In fact, I'm sure I haven't recognized many of them along the way.

The daily affirmations became such a part of the fabric of my existence, they were as necessary as eating a meal. And so it was, one day I received word that the community college in La Crosse, Wisconsin, was searching for an executive director for their foundation. The duties included fund-raising, marketing, and public relations, all of which fit my areas of expertise. So I applied for the position and was called in for an interview. I was told I was in fast company, as several of the other applicants were former community college presidents.

Members of the Search Committee consisted of six of the college's top administrators. Three of the members were very important, in my mind, because I thought their vote would carry the most weight regarding the hiring decision. The first was president of the college, the second was the vice president of student enrollment, and the third was an administrator from the health sciences area. All three were women and all were highly educated and very bright. Evidently I interviewed well; I was offered the position, which I accepted.

During the first interview meeting I had been introduced to the administrator from the health sciences area, Ms. Margarita Hayes. Maggie, as she was known, had the ability to light up a room whenever she entered. When we first met, I looked at her and stared at her blue eyes. I noticed they were filled with a depth of understanding and a sense of peace I hadn't ever seen in anyone else's eyes. I know it sounds funny and maybe even a little strange, but I felt I could see forever in her eyes. It was truly an *aha* moment and I knew there was a bond between us even though I had just met her. Unlike my younger years, however, I knew I didn't have to dwell on it because something special was there. I had learned to trust that if a special relationship was meant to be, it would come to pass.

As I became familiar with my surroundings and all that the job entailed, I met a number of other professionals on the staff. Several administrators had formed a loosely organized noontime runners club which I joined. Lo and behold, Maggie Hayes was a member of the club! I wouldn't miss a day of running with the group for any reason, just so I could spend some time with her, even if it was for a brief run. On several occasions, only two people showed up to run: Maggie and me.

We jogged together for about a year and it became obvious that Maggie and I liked each other a great deal. We solidified an honest friendship. We seemed to have many things in common and enjoyed hanging out together because we liked each other's company a lot. And so, it was after a Friday afternoon run that I asked her if she wanted to go out for a pizza the same evening.

She said yes.

*   *   *

When we decided to get serious about our relationship, we sat down to explore what each of us wanted most out of it. Maggie had recently experienced a divorce as well, so we both were going into it with our eyes wide open and cautious about the other person's behavior regarding all aspects of a relationship. We both expressed a concern that this was the first serious encounter for each of us after our divorces; the "rebound syndrome" was prominent in our minds.

We did something that has held us in good stead over the years. Each of us had a legal pad and a pencil. We went into different rooms of the house to write down the things we wanted from a new relationship—any relationship. We each came up with items that were near and dear to us. Interestingly enough, we had similar items on our lists, and while there weren't any great surprises, the exercise made several points clear to us.

The items on our lists were sacred to us. It was up to each of us to understand and accept those items, all of them, without exceptions.

They included promises to be made and promises to be kept, without question. As I reflect on those things now, the most important aspect of the exercise was that we'd listed items that are things that cause people to become irritated with their partner over time. We were concerned about those seemingly "little" things that build resentment until a relationship unravels. We agreed that nothing on those lists was too little or inconsequential to mention and discuss.

Our lists included things such as building a trusting relationship; not keeping secrets from one another; and being kind, gentle, and considerate with each other, without sarcasm or mockery. I wanted a sailboat and she agreed that we'd work together to make it a reality, while my commitment to her was to help her raise her ten-year-old daughter.

We discussed and agreed on other things not listed here. I'm sure most couples have their own concerns and issues to work through, but the things mentioned above pretty much sum up what we discussed and wanted from each other as we planned to share our lives together.

Each of us was committed to our relationship being the best it could be, so we decided early on to explore what we needed, pay attention to all the things we discussed, and keep our word with each other. The bottom line is that we found it all came down to trust. We had complete and unconditional trust in each other from the very beginning.

Don't get me wrong. We've had moments when we had to reconnect with our dreams, promises, and agreements, but that's not so hard to do when there is such mutual respect. The bond formed between us was a friendship based on trust. That trust was, and still is, a sacred promise between us.

Maggie has several intriguing qualities that to this day impress me. She has incredibly high integrity and is honest beyond measure. When she enters a room her charisma lights the room and people are automatically drawn to her. She is humble and yet proud, but not in an egotistical way. She's kind and extremely gracious to others. If she's offended by someone, they'll never know it because she won't embarrass anyone by telling them they caused her a "slight." She's too kind to hurt anyone. Her high energy is contagious and her sense of humor is great. I believe that who I am now matches very closely to who she is, which makes for a great relationship.

An insight gained: *People arrive in our lives at various moments to teach us a lesson or lessons. If we look for them, we'll find that great wisdom and* *insight can be gained from them. I believe that our time here on earth is a time of learning. This is in fact a giant classroom, and we are both students and teachers at any given moment.*

My belief is that a friendship involves a number of very important aspects. It begins with two people having a genuine sense of caring for each other. It means that in the good times, the relationship is mostly peaceful and loving. But it is in the difficult times, and there *will* be those times, that we remind ourselves to have the courage to explore new ways of making changes in our lives. A friend will listen to you, will disagree with you, but in the end, because of a genuine, nonjudgmental love and respect for each other, the two of you will come back to that loving place you share together.

Maggie and I have grown together emotionally over the years and it has been a blessing for me to have experienced that growth in myself and in her.

Many people seem to be on a quest to find a soul mate. It would be easy for me to say that Maggie and I felt we were soul mates from the first time we met, but I don't think that's accurate. Finding your mate is truly a spiritual event, and I believe it requires living and working through trials and tribulations to some degree. The challenges allow us to mature and grow together. Maggie and I have done that and we *are* soul mates.

Earlier in the book I mentioned that teachers come in various colors, shapes, and sizes. My first wife and I came through our young adult years and grew up together. We shared a great deal and I learned a lot from her, for which I am forever grateful.

However, the loss of Dan "brought the curtain down," if you will, with a trauma that I just could not overcome. Instead of moving in the same direction, we moved away from one other, each desperately trying to regain our emotional and spiritual footing. We both suffered from that trauma and our behavior showed it.

An insight gained: *When a relationship is built on caring and trust, both of the partners ought to assist the other to grow in areas that will bring them greater self-awareness for positive change. I don't think it is particularly* *healthy to go through time together without some challenges. For instance, if one of the partners comes from a family system that had impressed upon them that standing up for one's beliefs was frowned on, then the other partner might offer a chance to help the other person learn how to voice their opinions about various things without fear of recrimination. Two people in a friendship can truly be help mates.*

With the advent of the new beginning between Maggie and me, a new dynamic emerged. Having survived the battle and traumatic experiences that brought me to a greater awareness of my spiritual being, I had the scars to show for it.

Maggie and I looked forward to a loving relationship that would withstand the challenges and growth steps we knew would come our way. A great surprise was a birthday gift from Maggie—a sixteen-foot sailboat that we both learned how to sail.

I began to realize that my part in having a mutually successful relationship would mean I had to change the deep-seated feelings that almost destroyed me when Dan made his transition to the spirit world.

First on the list was my need to release Dan, with the knowledge that he came into the world to share his gifts and his life. He had been that "blade of grass" he wanted to be and had given of himself willingly as a source of energy, hope, and love to others. His mission was accomplished and he left nothing undone.

Memory flashback: A number of months ago, Maggie and I attended an alumni reunion at Cotter High School in Winona, MN, where Dan was a student. On this particular day, even though a number of years had passed since Dan's death, the school was holding a memorial service for both Dan and another student who had passed away.

A beautiful bench near the entrance of the high school was being dedicated in their memory. Several of Dan's classmates came to me and wanted to make sure I knew they were still thinking about him and that he'd impacted their lives in a powerful and positive way. They mentioned his gift of laughter, the achievements he'd accomplished as a swimmer, and what an inspiration he was to them during his final year in battling the cancer. It was clear to me that Dan gave those young people a light that still burns brightly in their hearts. It was a great testimony for me to hear that his purpose and his gifts still lived on in the minds of those students.

I've wondered at times if Dan's legacy would have been different had he lived a longer life. Probably yes, it would have been. But my reality now is that while he was sad when he told me on that Saturday night so many years ago that he wouldn't be able to be the "blade of grass" that he wanted to be, he has been that, and more.

He transformed my life. It became apparent to me it was time to awaken from the bad dream that was mine for so many years. My anger at God and the Catholic Church had been all consuming. Reciting those affirmations had a positive impact. My spirituality was deeper and richer than it had ever been before. Concepts started to make sense, where before I'd given them merely a passing thought. The most telling awareness that I had was centered on the notion of "cause and effect."

For years I couldn't, or wouldn't, grasp what that meant. But it's relatively simple. Basically, when you set something in motion, there will be some sort of response. It might be positive or it might prove to be negative. For instance, you can balance your checkbook by intuition or use the preferred method, which is to do the math and come up with the *real* numbers. Amazing how that works! (Smile.)

Dan's purpose was clear to me and I began to see that I needed to add some form and function to my own spirituality. I needed to figure out my own reason for being.

Anger was replaced with gentleness and peacefulness, along with the understanding and awareness that I could forgive myself for any and all failings, real or perceived. It allowed me to open my mind, to open my very being to love.

I realized that hope is real. It's the foundation from which anyone can launch an inspired way of viewing the events and challenges we bring into our lives.

An insight gained: *Free will is a gift that each of us has. The tricky part is making choices that are life giving and helpful to us on our journey through life.*

This was difficult to grasp in the beginning because I wanted to blame someone, mostly God, for the events I'd experienced in my life. In reality, it is usually the choices we make that result in the events we experience.

* * *

From the book, *Simple and Profound*, by the Joseph Collective, the spirit guides who were channeled through Susan Burns, with editorial guidance from Judith Struck, it states:

> *If you truly wish to be awakened but think you have not experienced it, look at other areas of your existence. If you are in fear in any area of your existence you will not be able to experience what you think of as awakening. Awakening is being without fear in all areas of your existence. When you awaken you are open to more energy and understanding love becomes easier. Do you see how important it is to gather energy? It allows you to take all that you have asked for from the universe. Look where it has been offered and where you have not taken it. Move fear away to make space for love. You then set up a conscious step toward the Creator because you are creating in that moment. To be enlightened means accepting what the Creator has given.*

Chapter Eleven
Winds of Change

*"When you commit to a spiritual partnership with another human being,
you bring the energy of the archetype of spiritual partnership into the
physical arena. You begin to form and to live by the values, perceptions,
and actions that reflect equality with your partner and a commitment to
his or her spiritual development and your own."*
—Gary Zukav, from *The Seat of the Soul*

Maggie and I had a true "meeting of the minds" in that we both agreed we were equals in the relationship. The magic of our friendship was forged and our new time together was one built on trust and caring for each other as equals.

A relationship doesn't really work if only one of the partners does all the work. I once believed that a successful marriage meant it was a fifty-fifty proposition, each giving 50 percent. But I suspect that isn't true, and a powerful, permanent, strong relationship requires 100 percent from each partner.

Maggie helped me tremendously when it came to making time for visits with my other sons. Tim attended the University of Minnesota to finish his master's degree in mathematics. Matthew and Michael went to the College (now University) of St. Thomas, in Saint Paul, Minnesota. Several trips back and forth across the United States, from Bermuda to Minneapolis, helped keep my sons and me in touch as a family, even though the strain of the divorce colored our relationship.

Memory flashback: When Grace and I separated, my son, Michael, had a very hard time with it, so I asked if he could find some time when the two of us could enjoy an extended visit. We decided to visit my sister, Marion, and brother-in-law, Bennie, in Tucson, Arizona. I flew to Chicago to meet him and we drove to Arizona. It was dubbed our "road trip of bonding." It's amazing how much can be accomplished when sharing thoughts, hopes, and fears in the confines of an automobile, driving across the country. It worked wonders for us and we, to this day, reflect back on that experience.

There was another time, shortly after the divorce was finalized and during a Christmas vacation break, when we were all missing each other for the holidays. The three boys and I decided it would be "high adventure" for us to pile into the big family sedan and drive from Minnesota to New Orleans, Louisiana, for a week. We had a ball. Again, it turned out to be a time of great sharing, of understanding, and most of all, forgiveness. The remarkable aspect of that trip was how kind we were to each other. There wasn't a need to blame anyone for what had happened between their mother and me. We all matured on that trip.

An insight gained: *Richard Bach, in his book, "Illusions: The Adventures of a Reluctant Messiah," stated that the only responsibility we have in this lifetime is to be happy. So, it's up to us to make ourselves happy. Everything else comes after that: God, spouse, family, job, etc. At the end of the day, you might say to yourself, "What did I do today that made me happy?" Hopefully you can find or name something that did make you happy. A daily self-inventory can be a good thing.*

The days rolled on and my work at the college took a turn in a direction that I struggled with. For so many years my consulting business gave me a tremendous measure of freedom in a busy schedule and also kept me out of the political and ego-driven dynamics inherent in a corporate structure. As I started to assess what a good and proper next step might be, one that fit my skills and experience, an opportunity presented itself that seemed too good not to pursue. I was also thinking that a geographical relocation was best for me, even though the counselors at Hazelden preached that such a move shouldn't be made for at least a couple of years after leaving a treatment program.

I always had my recovery in the Twelve Step Program as the basis for all the decisions I was going to make that affected my future.

Someone had given me an ad announcing a fund-raising position for a chief development officer at the Bermuda Biological Station for Research, in Bermuda. *Wow*, I said to myself, *that could be very exciting.* It was certainly far away from all that I knew, living in the Midwest. My undergraduate degree is in marine biology, I was a professional fund-raiser by trade, and sailing was a serious pursuit. If I was offered the position, I would definitely consider it was time for a geographical change.

That line of thinking didn't make much sense to many people, including Maggie. We were, after all, in a great relationship. The problem for me was that living in the same town where my ex-wife lived gave me great angst. It seemed, although it probably wasn't so, that every other day, whenever I was out jogging, she drove by. It really got to me after a while.

I approached Maggie and asked if we could work through the notion of change, that is, my leaving La Crosse, Wisconsin, to go to Bermuda on my own for a period of time. I know I asked for a great deal, and after much honest, caring discussion, she agreed we could make it work. Maggie's love is awesome and her friendship is pure and honest. I know how blessed I am to have found her.

Fate played another role in my decision and I did get the offer; the only problem was that to leave Maggie was difficult. After making the decision to be in a long-distance relationship with Maggie, I was also struggling trying to figure out how to stay close to my sons even though I was ready for a big new adventure in Bermuda.

As the plane lifted off the ground at JFK Airport in New York City in a slight rain, I was wondering if I had made the correct decision to leave everyone behind.

Since I'd rarely traveled out of the United Sates, I wondered what life would be like in a foreign country. My excitement grew as our plane began to bank toward the east when the approach to runway 16 came into view. I gazed down on the small island paradise which had seemed so far away on the map, awed by the surrounding turquoise sea that almost looked fake—as though someone had dropped a tanker-load of food coloring into the water.

After the plane landed and I made my way through customs, I enjoyed the warmth of a beautiful island bathed in the golden glow of the setting sun.

After four months of being separated, Maggie and I decided we wanted to spend our lives together and not remain apart. Subsequently, she quit her job, sold her house in Wisconsin, and came to Bermuda. It was our good fortune that Maggie was hired by the Bio-Station as the director of education. So we were both employed by the Bermuda Biological Station for Research, which is an offshore oceanographic facility similar to Woods Hole in Massachusetts and/or Scripps in California.

In our former lives, we'd both forged family traditions with our other families. All families have them and they generally center on events like birthdays, children's milestones and accomplishments, vacations, holidays, and buying homes. It was time that Maggie and I formed some new traditions of our own. It began with our move to the islands. We spent three years living in a new country, working and playing in an island paradise.

Each of us had a "history" that served as a constant reminder that our new relationship put us in the "newbie" category, so to speak.

We were anxious to make our own history, all the while realizing it would take years to achieve. A funny memory we have is the time we purchased a Christmas tree that was shipped from Canada to Bermuda. We didn't know that the steamship had to sit in quarantine for several months before the trees could be offloaded onto the island. The tree looked great at first, but I could tell it was fragile when I put it in the stand and Maggie began to decorate it. The decorations were pretty and unique, to say the least; Maggie had found island creatures such as starfish, mollusks, and other assorted seashells, and spray-painted them silver and gold. We had a truly "island" Christmas tree.

The next day we woke up to find that 90 percent of the pine needles had fallen off the branches, and the decorations had gone with them. Evidently, being quarantined for so long without being watered did the Canadian trees in. That's the first and only time I ever saw a bald Christmas tree.

Another real eye-opener was when Maggie went into Hamilton, the capital of Bermuda, to initiate having telephone service installed in our cottage. She was promptly told that she couldn't sign us up, since only the man of the house could arrange the service. We later found out that Bermuda was granted its freedom and independence from England in 1962 and was still trying to bring equality to its society. On another note, while Bermuda does not have a caste system per se, it was obvious to us there was some sort of unwritten pecking order in their society. Despite the order placing American expats at the lowest rung on the ladder, the Bermudian culture is marvelous because of the courtesy everyone shows each other, and to this day we have made that a part of our way of living.

* * *

While I worked in my area of expertise as a professional fund-raiser, many lessons unfolded. A different set of rules governed Bermuda's process of asking for "gift income," which is, basically, unrestricted money in support of a nonprofit organization similar to the Bermuda Biological Station, which I represented. The biggest revelation to me was how, as a development professional, we formed strategic relationships with high-net-worth individuals. In the USA, I cultivated potential donors and then, if it was appropriate, asked the person for a donation. But in Bermuda, the key was to determine *who* the best person would be to ask for a gift. The development person would *never* be the one asking for money. The "dance" was, so to speak, to have a volunteer do the bidding for an organization. This translated into spending most of my time cultivating the volunteers first. Then when appropriate, I'd arrange the time and the venue for the volunteer to ask an interested person for a "gift."

Our years in Bermuda defined us as a couple, and since the island is only sixty-two miles long and a mile wide at its widest point, all Type A personalities learn quickly that mental and emotional survival depends on how quickly one can slow down their personal pace.

Bermuda exudes peace, tranquility, and exquisite beauty. The pink beaches offer days of relaxation in the warm Bermuda sunshine. I partook when time permitted, after job, family, and other commitments. Living in a new country, a new society, and meeting new people, most of whom were not American, was indeed challenging.

The biggest opportunity to grow for me, however, was helping to parent Megan, who was Maggie's ten-year-old daughter. I'd had a lot of experience in helping to raise four boys, but I knew nothing about raising girls and, sure enough, the lessons came quickly.

In comparison, boys are easier to raise because when they act up, you call them aside, lay the law down in no uncertain terms, and they suck it up and move on. The tension is over as soon as it started.

This is not so with a girl. When she acted up, I would call her aside and lay down the law. Then I would stand around for hours wondering why all she did was cry because her feelings were hurt.

I received some great advice from my secretary one day when I arrived at the office, still upset with an episode at home. She said, "Hank, when Megan and her mother get into an argument or disagreement, do the right thing and leave the room to let them work it out between them." Absolutely the best advice I ever had.

An insight gained: *Those who come into our lives as teachers come in all types of "packages." The physical package isn't important; it's the subject matter of what is to be taught and might be learned that counts. Some of the best lessons I've learned have come from people who absolutely bothered me. In fact, several of those folks were people I didn't want to be around ... although, in retrospect, the lessons I learned from them turned out to be exactly what was needed at that moment. I learned not to judge by outward appearances. I received sage advice many years ago from my friend, Bill, which I've never forgotten: "If you look into people's eyes, and look into their soul, you would look beyond their physical bodies, and you would see their true being." To learn how to see people on a "soul level" instead of the outward appearance before you, is a challenge, to say the least. But it allows you to put aside your judgment of others. Amen to that.*

* * *

Life in Bermuda was also a great transition time that separated me from my former life and surroundings. It's often said that making a geographical change is not the best thing to do after difficult life situations have occurred.

I don't entirely agree with that. I think it may have to do with when and why you decide to relocate. Moving to Bermuda the week after Dan's death would have been the worst thing for me to do, but doing it when and how I did, made the move the best thing that could have happened. I was intent on keeping all of my relationships intact and worked hard at being the best dad I could possibly be.

Maggie and I eventually were married in Bermuda. Megan was able to spend her summer months with us so we, in effect, had a new family dynamic. The real challenge for me was keeping in touch with my three sons back in the States. I never wanted them to feel abandoned by me. Though we all had our moments of tension, we worked through them graciously.

Eventually, Maggie and I made the transition, and it came to pass that spending weekends on the pink beaches, riding around the island on a moped bike, and running in road races and triathlons wasn't all that hard to take.

The spiritual significance of my time in Bermuda involved meditation on a deep level and the elimination of all the financial obligations that once weighed heavily on my psyche and our purse strings.

In the early morning hours, I would sit on the veranda of our cottage overlooking the Atlantic Ocean, and meditate. I was greeted with cool balmy weather as the sun came into the eastern sky. The lavender shades of the sky slowly gave way to the warmth of a blazing sun by noon.

Serenity and harmony slowly replaced the negative thoughts and patterns I'd brought into my previous existence.

An insight gained: *The Source of life is the light of God. You may call it your Higher Power, Allah, Christ, The One. I believe the name doesn't matter because the Kingdom of God is within us. We needn't look outside of ourselves—everything we need is contained in us. The Creator put it there in the first place. The Holy Spirit is alive and well and lives within us, and is* *present to help us on our journey. When in doubt, ask for help from the Holy Spirit. There is no failure rate . . . we always get what we need. We may not get what we want, but in time we will know the answer. Joseph, a spirit guide, beckons us to simply ask, "Creator, show me love," and it comes post-haste.*

* * *

I could see the changes expressed in my joy for life, along with my sense of humor and self-confidence. Americans who work in a foreign country are called expats and the United States government allows a significant tax break because we work in a foreign country. And, by living frugally, we actually saved money, the first time for me in many, many moons.

Our move back to the States was inevitable and with Megan's high school years quickly approaching, Maggie and I made plans to relocate again. The child custody aspect with Megan's dad changed since she now spent the school year with us and summers with him.

A dear friend, Steven, an executive recruiter in Stamford, Connecticut, placed me in a position at Manhattan College in New York City. Maggie was hired by New York University, and we bought a home in Tarrytown, New York. We became acclimated to life in New York, and within two years Maggie finished her doctoral degree at Fordham University in the Bronx.

During that time, Steven Ast asked me to assist him with an executive search at Northwestern University. I agreed to do it, and it went so well that I was brought into the firm as vice president and senior executive recruiter. What a pleasant turn of events! I spent three years learning the executive search trade and became good at being an executive recruiter. That experience launched a new career for me and, thankfully, I thrived in the executive search industry.

At that point in my spiritual journey I continued to meditate and stay focused on my affirmations. I found an ashram in nearby Yorktown Heights, New York, and was able to reconnect with people who made daily meditation a part of their lives.

I was continuing to change and I could sense that all the internal work I was doing was beginning to pay dividends. My spirit guides were active and, as I reflect back now, I had many things to be thankful for.

An insight gained: *I believe the opposite of love is not hate, it's indifference. When we argue with someone, it means that on some level we care, even if we think we hate them. Otherwise we would be indifferent and simply walk away, not caring to continue the argument. Indifference is hurtful because it basically tells us that in the eyes of someone else, we really don't exist. Learning how (and it takes practice) to forgive ourselves is the first step, and the only step that will allow us to forgive others. Forgiving ourselves leads to loving ourselves. Only then are we free to love others.*

Megan graduated from Sleepy Hollow High School and attended the Coast Guard Academy for her freshman year. Wanting something different in her life, she transferred to the University of Rhode Island where she earned a degree in chemical engineering.

Our family was growing and maturing. After graduating from the University of St. Thomas in Saint Paul, Minnesota, with a degree in marketing, Matthew married and began building his family of two daughters with his wife, Trisha. Shortly after, Michael finished his doctorate in sociology at Loyola University in Chicago, got married, and is raising a daughter with his wife, Amelia. Tim was finishing a second master's degree, in computer science, at the University of Minnesota, and was married after the other two boys, and he and his wife, Barbara, have a son. Megan and Guy were the last to marry and have two daughters.

The winds of change started to blow once again for Maggie and me. Megan and the boys had new careers, and Maggie and I looked at each other and thought the same thing . . . why not go where the weather suits our clothes—down south.

We thought we'd buy another sailboat and enjoy the warmer climate, and that's exactly how it came to pass.

Maggie was hired by the Florida Community College System (now State College System) in Jacksonville, Florida. I was the "trailing spouse" this time. Remember that equality discussion Maggie and I had early on?

We put that into practice. Earlier in the year I'd talked to Steven and his partner at the search firm. I suggested that I launch a southern office for them. It didn't spark any great interest for them.

So, I did what every true-blooded American entrepreneur would do, I started my own executive search firm. At first I wasn't sure how to get started. However, with some study, some guidance from Steve, a little bit of chutzpah, and some assistance from an active group of spirit guides, it all came together. In the twelve years we've been in business, and with several monster years of growth, our firm is still going strong.

An insight gained: *As I write this book, I've found a way to bring peace into my life. I realize, now more than ever, that all my experiences up to this point—the good, the difficult, and especially the very difficult—have made me who and what I am today. I'm truly blessed with the guidance I've received from so many people, both here on this plane we call earth and from those in the spirit world.*

Chapter Twelve

Important Decisions

"We can't imagine what life would be like without meditation. It has seen us through tough times and many life changes, keeping us sane and grounded and real. Life is challenging enough; we can never know what will arise next and only when our minds are clear and focused can we make the best decisions. How are you able to deal with the madness and chaos that occurs daily? How do you deal with the challenges of life? Meditation is highly misunderstood and often underrated yet is perhaps what it takes to be a truly sane person."
—Ed and Deb Shapiro: *How Your Attitude Gives You Altitude!*

I n his excellent book, *How to Meditate,* Paul Roland states:

"It is a common misconception that meditation and conventional forms of relaxation are the same thing. However, meditation is not the passive act that it appears, and when practiced regularly it has the potential to bring far greater benefits than simple relaxation. While relaxation offers temporary relief from stress, meditation aims to achieve both relaxation of the body and a heightened state of awareness. Regular meditation can bring greater control over restless thoughts and emotions, leading to a sense of wellbeing."

I agree totally with Roland's statement, and the following is how and what I did to reinvent myself by incorporating a system of meditation.

If you've read this book from the beginning, you know some of the events that spurred me to make a definitive and positive change in my life.

I have been through some incredibly trying times, some of which I'm not proud of at all. But, then again, as I assess my life in retrospect, I can only surmise that it all had to happen the way it did, to get me to where I am today.

I'm proud of where I am and who I am today, and I'm not talking about an ego-based pride. I'm happy and thankful every day for the quality of life, joy, and peace that I have in my life. When I look back at where I was when I began my spirit journey, I'm humbled that I've come so far.

Believe me, the work that got me here was darn hard. But it worked for me, and my hope is that a similar process may work for you. So, the bottom line for me is, if you can reap some benefit from reading about the process that brought this significant change into my life, then indeed this information has accomplished one of my goals. Perhaps it will help and encourage you to make changes in your life.

What is my other goal in writing this book? I've had a chance to review my life, and the process has provided me a great sense of renewal.

The first decision I made was to recover from my grief. It took some time, but eventually I realized I didn't want to stay stuck in my grief. I knew I couldn't change the past, but I could control whether or not I'd continue to give the past the power to control me. I could keep my history and be stuck with the pain, or I could choose to release it from my life and move forward to transcend the grief and loss. I had the choice to move beyond the perceived pain, or I could hold on to sadness, which in fact only created more sadness and didn't allow any room for healing to take place. By the way, I believe now that this is what free will allows.

The second decision I made was to begin to meditate on a *daily* basis. This was the biggest hurdle to overcome, yet it served as the basis of support during my healing and continues to be a source of peace and strength to this day. Once, I was asked what would happen if I stopped meditation after experiencing peace and serenity from meditating. It's very easy for life and commitments to push your meditation schedule aside. The reasons we stop meditating, or exercising, or doing things that are good for us, aren't important, really. My thought is that this is similar to knitting a sweater. As you knit the sweater during the day, you make great progress. Then unbeknownst to you, someone, during the wee hours, steals in and unravels the progress you made on the sweater that day. You made progress, and then it slips away. Certainly, this is a simplistic metaphor. However, the idea is that if you spend so much time and energy working to change old habits that at one time were not healthy, why throw away that investment and let your mind return to your old ways of thinking? We now know that incorrect thinking drives incorrect behavior. So for me, I keep "knitting," no matter what comes up.

The key was an unwavering **commitment** to stay with whatever meditation process I believed would work best. I knew that without such a commitment to do the work, it would slowly unravel and fade away. The distractions in life are immense and it's easy to set aside a practice that takes us into the unknown and forces us to confront the difficult things in our life.

The second most important step was internalizing the meaning and value of the affirmations I used on a daily basis. My affirmations came from reading the works of Louise Hay which, in my mind, were unparalleled to bring about significant change.

My reality was that I had many obstacles to overcome, and if I was to keep my sanity I needed to find a way to bring peace into my life. I read somewhere that we are the only ones who can guard the entrance to our minds. I really like that idea because we live in an information age that is changing at warp speed and with it comes great change in how we receive positive information.

Unfortunately, we are also bombarded by an avalanche of information from so-called experts or high-tech salesmen about what drugs to take, foods to eat, clothes to wear, weight to get to, or career to attain. While it's good to be informed, our opinions of self, peace, quality, values, morality, religion, and everything else are impacted by the blitz day in and day out. It also affects our ability to slow down enough to listen to ourselves think.

An insight gained: *We serve ourselves well if we can step back and view who we are from a vantage point outside ourselves. In doing so, I became aware of* *myself as I developed the ability to sense what drove my thoughts, feelings, and actions. Practicing the birds-eye view of myself showed me that my ego was in the driver's seat! Taking inventory or observing myself objectively gave me an understanding of who I was. However, let me be quick to say that I didn't always like what I saw. That served all the more as an incentive to make significant changes in my life.*

*   *   *

My point is this: It is up to us to control and manage the information we receive from the world outside. It was important when I considered reinventing myself. To be the master of my own life, rather than live a life dictated by ego and old patterns and thoughts, demanded that I had to train myself to think and act on all the information presented to me. No one can deny that our society is fraught with many ills and systems that simply don't make sense. In addition, we live in an advanced society with many great attributes that help us. So I began to realize that if I was to successfully "reinvent" myself, then I needed to "re-school" myself regarding how I accepted and processed information. Once again, a commitment to peace and joy was critical to this process. Without that, the process seems too hard and the goals too lofty.

Because I'm a creature of habit, it was difficult to move away from old ways of doing things and old ways of thinking. That included how I perceived ideas, shaped my opinions, and how I thought change would come about. When things are familiar to us, they seem safer than delving into the unfamiliar, so we fight hard to hang on to what's familiar.

I continue to see this lesson demonstrated by watching people who cannot make a change for the better and remain in bad relationships. It doesn't seem to matter that they are being physically and/or emotionally abused in the relationship. It's frightfully difficult when a person has an alcoholic spouse and is being abused, especially if the abuser spouse is providing most of the financial support for the family.

The relationship is further complicated when the person being abused is an enabler and thus actually fosters the abusing spouse's bad behavior by allowing it. It's a catch-22 and takes a strong-willed person with a solid support structure to make a change in their life. Enablers are often dealing with their own self-esteem issues, and seeking a way out is profound because they are so unsure of themselves and their abilities. It gets more overwhelming when children and finances are involved. While living a life in fear certainly isn't a healthy thing to do, change can be even more terrifying for some.

When I decided to reinvent myself for a better way of life, my alcoholic family experiences were not the only factor, by any stretch. I was trying to cope with the death of my son, a loss of faith in the religious structure I'd always relied on, and a business that failed. I couldn't help my wife with her grief either, and had to concede our marriage. I couldn't seem to find what I ought to be doing to fulfill my life's purpose.

Truly my desire was to move away from the life that was my current experience, one that was pain-filled, riddled with huge failures, and wasn't nurturing or fulfilling. It was time to rethink *how* I thought about myself. The good news was, there was a way to change. The not-so-good news was, in order to effect, or produce, change there was going to be difficult work ahead. I slowly began to realize there was only one person who could do it, however, and it was me.

In the Twelve Step Program, it's said that until a person feels enough intense pain from the things they have lost personally, they will not succeed on the path of recovering from the addictions they have. This also applies to anyone who thinks about making a change. No pain, no change. It takes a hell of a lot of personal courage to be someone new.

The third decision I made was to *name* what I wanted in my life. Writing down what really made sense to me was a big step. It seemed silly at first, because in the past my ideas were only thoughts kept somewhere in the depths of my mind. It was now time to dream big and to dream purposefully. To "dream my dream" was an important part of my process. It was, in effect, my road map.

Laying out all the fine points, for example, how soon I wanted something or how much it cost, was not part of this step. I asked my Higher Power to take care of the details, through sticking diligently to my daily affirmations. I was required to "dream the dream," giving space in my life for the dreams to be realized.

I had a support group and one person who could offer me help, because sharing my ideas with someone I trusted let me know that my push for change was all right as long as I didn't do it at the expense of anyone else. Also, supportive people offered assistance in times of doubt and gave me an avenue to express my feelings and frustrations. Strong support enabled me to seek direction when loneliness came knocking and I doubted the process and myself. Many times, moments of self-doubt came like a "thief in the night," and I believe it was part of the learning curve to find and fashion myself into the person I wanted to be.

So, to effect the changes, the notes to myself included things such as the following:

- I wanted, once and for all, to have peace and serenity. I was tired of a life filled with jumbled thinking. The affirmation I used was: "I release all fear, as I am worthy of living a life filled with peace and harmony."
- I wanted to find a mate who would be the best for me, as I continued through the rest of the years on this journey. For this part, my affirmation was simple: "I am worthy of being in a loving relationship."
- Next, my family was a major concern since the split family could have lasting negative effects on my children. I asked diligently for healing, and my affirmation was this: "I ask for a loving family, one blessed with love and caring for each other."
- The failed business always weighed on my mind and my self-confidence took a mighty blow. Again my affirmation was simply put out there: "I am worthy of having and running a successful business based on best practices."
- Owning a beautiful oceangoing sailboat was prominent as well. I used the affirmation: "I am worthy of having a beautiful, safe, cruising sailboat."

The power to all of these affirmations was, once again, the fact that I recited them every day over and over.

In his book titled *The Outliers: The Story of Success*, Malcolm Gladwell discusses the professional lives of several people who became incredibly successful in their chosen fields of endeavor because they practiced skills relating to the work they were involved in. He mentions that the success they enjoyed came about because they spent over 10,000 hours working at tasks that proved to take them above and beyond the ordinary.

The same holds true with this area of reinventing oneself. I'm sure I invested over 10,000 hours in my affirmations.

The fourth and final decision was to learn the how-to of a meditation form that made sense to me. Why meditation? Simply put, I needed a way, a system, or a method that opened the channels of dialogue between my Higher Power and me.

I'd read many books over many months, and they all pointed to the concept that the power of the universe, through one's Higher Power, was waiting and willing to assist each of us in achieving what we want in life. It took a great deal of practice, and I actually had to convince myself that it was okay for me to ask for what I wanted.

Through daily meditation, the stage was set: that which I asked for, was clear and without pause or hesitation.

An excellent book on this subject is *Ask and It Is Given: Learning to Manifest Your Desires*, by Esther and Jerry Hicks. Esther is a channel for the spirit guide called Abraham. Asking is the easy part; knowing what to ask for and being consistent with asking is the difficult part.

Meditation has allowed me to have some great insights into ideas and awareness that have at times really surprised me.

Memory flashback: One afternoon not too long ago I was riding in an airplane, traveling from Minneapolis, Minnesota, to Chicago, Illinois.

I was seated in the rear of the plane mindlessly looking at the passengers in front of me, and decided to use the time to meditate. Upon going deep into a meditative state, I began to sense something strange and had the distinct feeling that it seemed odd we were all being hurtled through time and space, not really knowing anything about it. I imagined what it would be like for someone 300 years ago to be sitting on the plane as I was. I became aware that we were all wrapped up in our own worlds, consumed with our own thoughts, and living out our existence the best way each of us knew how. Certainly we were oblivious to each others' worlds.

Nonetheless, I slowly opened my eyes and noticed it was still a cloudless afternoon with beautiful sunshine opening up an incredible vista of the earth. From my window, I looked down on the world and saw we were flying over one of the northern suburbs of Chicago. I could see cars winding their way around the ribbons of roads.

I imagined that those thousands of people were also lost in their own worlds, consumed with their own thoughts, and living out their existence with their individual purposes. My mind flashed to the billions of people on earth and they, too, were consumed with their own worlds and existences. I wondered with great fascination if God really knew all of the thousands of souls who were below me and those on my airplane.

Did God have to work with and guide the lives of everyone who has incarnated onto this earthly plane of existence? This concept was impressed on me as a young boy growing up in the Catholic Church. I can still hear the nun saying, "Better be a good boy. After all, God is watching you. He knows everything you do." So at that point, the thoughts still came flooding through, even as I continued trying to throw off some of those ideas that I now believe to be sophomoric and childish.

*   *   *

I started to think about myself, and wondered: Who fashioned my purpose in life? Is it truly my free will that drives me from a place of darkness to a place of light and love? Do I control that which I seek to be? How do I find my way toward being a more complete person? The answers did eventually come to me, and it was on a sailboat in the middle of the Atlantic Ocean.

My sailing mates were working or dozing below as I monitored the autopilot system that was working beautifully. With a calm sea and very little breeze we were sailing quietly through deep-blue ocean waters, headed for the Florida coast.

Looking out over the bow of the boat, a thin line suggested that the horizon was far off in the distance. From port to starboard to aft of the boat my eyes followed that thin line 180 degrees. The ocean was vast, dark, and seemed eerily endless. I was in awe because I felt so small and insignificant. I knew in reality that if I could have viewed myself from six miles above the boat, I would realize how insignificant I really was. The boat would be a mere speck on the ocean. What a blow to my ego, as my importance in this world seemed so much greater than that.

I closed my eyes for a moment and looked inward. Searching deep inside my psyche, I found it was indeed my soul that I walked with in a vastness far exceeding anything the ocean had to offer. My inner being went on and on, and truly the feeling was as though I could see forever. Eternity seemed so close. A chill swept over my body and I slowly opened my eyes to see a majestic orange sun setting peacefully in the western sky. I thought back to that plane ride I had taken months before and realized that the depth of my soul held the answer. All the answers were, in fact, inside me.

I could be whoever I wanted to be, with the free will given to me by my Creator, to do all things. All I had to do was ask for help.

Chapter Thirteen

Meditation

To dream the impossible dream ... To fight ... the unbeatable foe ...
To bear ... with unbearable sorrow ... To run ... where the brave dare
not go ... To right ... the unrightable wrong ... To love ... pure and
chaste from afar ... To try ... when your arms are too weary ...
To reach ... the unreachable star.
Lyrics from the song, "The Impossible Dream"
(The Quest) written by Joe Darion

Once the commitment is made to do it, daily meditations are relatively easy to build into our routine. Many practitioners meditate for ten to fifteen minutes a day, although some people meditate longer. But ten to fifteen minutes is probably all that is needed. The caution about meditation, like many things that make us feel good, is that it's easy to get caught up in the good feeling and it can become a crutch. Keeping it simple is best.

An experience I had while at The Christine Center in Wisconsin was a game changer. One of my final visits to the Center was a two-week intensive program called a "sensory deprivation" or "cave experience." It was two weeks of immersion in deep meditation and contemplation. For ten days our group meditated and prayed twelve to fourteen hours a day. (I do not suggest that everyone must do this, by the way.) We also went through a detoxification session which prohibited use of coffee, sugar, and bread. Then the real challenge came. For the last four days of the program we were given the option of taking the intensive "cave experience" or not. I opted to take it.

*   *   *

I entered a cabin that had been completely blacked out: the windows, the door, everything was completely devoid of light. The goal was to live in the cabin for two-and-a-half days without interruptions of any kind. No lights, no TV, no radio, and nothing to read. Complete darkness and isolation. It was called a "cave experience."

I went in on a Friday morning with the intention to emerge sometime on Sunday afternoon. All I had was a porta-potty to use, a bag of raw almonds, eight oranges, a gallon of water, eight bananas, and some whole wheat crackers.

At first it didn't seem as though it would be a difficult thing to do, but as the hours wore on I couldn't tell if it was night or day and started to feel a little strange. Of course, you could guess what the time was at first, but after a while that became more difficult as the hours started to run together.

In that blackened cabin, I meditated, prayed, sang, talked to myself, and cried. I argued with myself as I reviewed the events of the last forty years.

At first the conversations were one-way; however, somewhere in that time frame my communication with my son and others in the spirit world started to make sense. I gained insight into many things that I'd struggled with for many years. The demons I faced were mine and I had no choice but to meet them head-on.

It became obvious that blaming others was childish, powerless, and dishonest. It was an extreme purging of sorts that brought into focus new life and a new perspective of who I was. At some point, I guessed it was late Sunday morning, I emerged from the "cave" to be met by several members of the core group. My soul felt clean. The euphoria was almost overwhelming and the commitment to my new life was profound.

Reflection: The "cave experience" is not something everyone ought to go through. I am a Type A personality, and for me it was a challenge. I did learn a great deal about myself. I also gained insight as to a new direction for my life. It was another step in my growth process.

*   *   *

So here is the part in this book where most people want to know about results. What actually happened? What's the tale of the tape, so to speak?

Okay, so here's the way it is for me now:

- The inner peace that I feel, which is real, is a result of becoming more aware of who I am and how my ego drives my thinking. My self-awareness allows me to say to myself, *Let go of the fear that you feel. Accept love and forgiveness from the Holy Spirit.* Ask and it is given to you. It's that simple!
- My relationship with my beautiful second wife of twenty-four years is fantastic. Since we are both human, from time to time we have things to work through because that's part of a relationship between two people.
- Our family has never been more loving toward each other. We feel close and say "I love you" after our conversations on the phone or when we have to travel away from each other. When we're together in person, a big hug is automatic and heartfelt. We thrive on lots of hugs.
- I am currently the president and owner of a very successful national executive search firm in Florida, which I started thirteen years ago.
- I own, outright, a forty-three-foot Tartan sailboat which is capable of sailing around the world.
- The original dreams that I dreamt have been manifested, for which I am eternally thankful.

What I hope I'm doing here is giving you some sort of "proof" that all the hard work I brought into my life has resulted in the changes that I worked at and asked for.

The bottom line is, I truly believe that if *I* could do it, and I did, *so can you* if you work at it.

* * *

As I mentioned before, there is an "information overload" available at our fingertips. If you'd like to explore meditation, go to the Internet and key in the words "how to meditate" into your search engine. You'll have all the information you'll ever need on the subject.

The bottom line is this: There is no *right* way to meditate. The way that works best for you is the right way. Here are several hints to support you in your journey:

- Realize from the very beginning that you will be constantly distracted. It's a part of the process. Even experienced meditation practitioners have to deal with constant distractions.
- Find a quiet place where you'll have the fewest distractions. This might be a room in the house, or if you have a basement, go there and find a quiet spot.
- Wear comfortable clothing. Elastic waistbands and tight-fitting clothing might be a distraction. Even little things will become major distractions in a heartbeat.
- Dress warmly. Cold hands, cold feet, or the feeling that wind is blowing on your neck or face will distract you. Outdoor noises such as fans, lawn mowers, leaf blowers, etc., are some of the major detractors.
- Set a time frame for how long you want to meditate.
- If you should fall asleep when you first start learning to meditate, that's normal. Having several mantras or affirmations to repeat will help prevent it. If you're tired to begin with, it stands to reason that when you start to relax, you'll doze off.
- Your ego will bombard your brain with all kinds of thoughts. Again, very normal. Ignore your ego, it just wants to remind you that it thinks it's in charge.

- Your ego will tell you repeatedly that what you are doing is foolish! Keep meditating, and let the Holy Spirit come in.
- Reaffirm your commitment to practice daily. If you miss a day or two, be kind to yourself and start again.
- When your mind begins to wander, be gentle with yourself and come back to your original thought.
- If you can find a teacher as a guide, all the better.
- Read up on the subject and pay close attention to any pitfalls that might be suggested.
- Be open to speak to your spirit guides (and yes, we all have them). Some call them guardian angels. Having spirit guides is not a New Age concept. They are our help mates, and when you open up to hear what they have to tell you, amazing insights can be yours to enjoy.
- Knowing what to ask for and being consistent in asking for what you want, will come easier to you as you practice.

Chapter Fourteen

God Is Love

I think I can make it now, the pain is gone
All of the bad feelings have disappeared
Here is the rainbow I've been prayin' for
It's gonna be a bright (bright), bright (bright)
Sun-Shiny day.
Lyrics from "I Can See Clearly Now," by Johnny Nash

S everal years ago I thought being a hospice chaplain would be a great thing to do. I figured that if I wasn't in it for the long haul, certainly I would do it for a number of years.

It was not meant to be. I soon realized the gift of being a hospice caregiver rested squarely with people who are "called" to that profession. The time and training that I received were profound, however. And I'm delighted to share three experiences with you because they've meant so much to me in my journey.

A core group of chaplains and chaplains-to-be (I was in the latter group) met each morning at eight o'clock. We met five days a week for an hour a day.

At a Catholic Franciscan healthcare medical center where I worked, the facilitator, a Catholic nun, began each meeting with a prayer. The agenda that followed was simple. Each of us was encouraged to share any thoughts and/or feelings that we had regarding the work we were involved in over the past twenty-four hours. To set the stage correctly:

This was the first time I ever talked about my feelings as they related to assisting people who were getting ready to leave this earth.

* * *

My first memorable experience was with the chaplaincy program's facilitator.

"So Henry, how did you handle your visit with the elderly woman, Mrs. Jones, who passed away while you were holding her hand?" she asked me.

"I said all the prayers that I had at hand. I talked to her and gave her my blessings and tried to reassure her that she'd led a very productive life working on the family farm," I responded.

"Not good enough," the facilitator replied.

Though not devastated, I was bothered by her response, so I thought hard about what I could do differently. I was hard-pressed to come up with some better things to talk about the next time I spent time with someone in that situation.

As it turned out, I learned that hospice caregivers have to do their homework! If I was going to truly minister to people, I'd have to know something about them. Merely sitting with them was comforting enough, but that wasn't my role entirely. I needed to provide more for them.

It was also hard to explain my feelings, seeing as how she'd died right in front of me. I was dumbfounded by the director's question. The eventual purpose of the question was for all of us to understand and be comfortable with, as best we could, our own mortality.

So, in my own mind I had to decide if death was an ending of a journey or if death was a beginning of a new journey. The answer is reflected in how we "walk" with someone as they prepare for their transition into the spirit world.

The second experience was even more difficult for me. I was asked to visit with an elderly gentleman who was, I was told, in a coma and near death. I went into his room and stood by his bed. I introduced myself and told him that I knew his name and I was there to visit with him by saying several prayers.

This time I was better prepared; I knew about his family—his wife, kids, granddaughters—and the work he was involved in most of his life. I began by reciting the usual Catholic prayers to him. *Silence.*

I mentioned to him I thought he could hear me so I was delighted I could offer the prayers. I said them again. *Silence.*

I talked to him about his life and gave him my blessing. *Silence.*

I stood there not knowing what else to do or say. Finally, I thanked him for the opportunity to pray with him and told him I hoped I was of some comfort to him. I left the room feeling empty. I wanted to give more, but had nothing else to give him.

At the debriefing the following day, I was told I did all the right things. Somehow I'd expected it to feel different than it had, though.

This last experience was a game changer for me. I'm going to call this gentleman Fritz (not his real name). As chaplains, we had to pull "weekend duty" every fourth weekend. Our time began on Friday afternoon and lasted until early Monday morning when the shifts changed.

I visited with several families all day Friday and Saturday. I was trying my best to offer comfort and prayers to families who had members coming in and out of the emergency room. I was exhausted, but had to work all day Sunday as well. Thank goodness the evenings were somewhat peaceful, since we only had to respond to code blue situations, which usually meant to go post-haste to the intensive care unit.

I made it through Sunday and was sound asleep when the code blue came in around four o'clock Monday morning. I went to the ICU wing and was told that Mr. Fritz was not doing well. I went to his bedside and pulled the curtain around the bed so a young nurse and I could have some private time with Mr. Fritz.

His breathing was labored and raspy and he looked jaundiced. It was apparent that he would not be with us much longer. I began to recite the Lord's Prayer and just as I was about to finish, his breathing became louder and more pronounced. As I said "For Thine is the Kingdom and the Power," he stopped breathing, and I heard a faint "zip" and saw something faintly white leave his body.

I turned quickly to the nurse and said, "Did you see that?"

She said, "See what?"

I said, "Oh, never mind. I thought I saw something."

I went back to my room because it was now time to call it a weekend. After packing my things, I headed out to my car in the parking lot and noticed the sun was making its entrance into the world to start another day. I wanted sleep.

As I drove on Highway 61 and headed north along the Mississippi River, which reflected the sunlight, I was thinking I'd had the opportunity to be of assistance to a number of people. Then it hit me like a ton of bricks!

I shouted, "That's it! Holy cow, that's it . . . we have a soul!"

I pounded on the steering wheel in awe of the realization. That's what I saw and heard leave Mr. Fritz's body. I truly believed I was witness to something spectacular. I was overcome with joy. My goodness, what a revelation!

Chapter Fifteen

Choices

"Reaching the goal is not the only measure of success."
—H. R. Maly

Cause and effect: it's the phenomenon that makes the lessons I learned understandable.

The concept of thinking ahead—and by that I mean *planning ahead* to account for the results that might occur as a consequence of my actions or decisions—was an eye-opener. It reminds me of the saying, "If you hit your finger often enough when you're hammering a nail, sooner or later you figure out how to hold the nail so you don't hit your finger again."

I realize it is my responsibility to take charge of my life (learn how to hold the nail). It isn't up to anyone else.

I've experienced much pain. It was a great teacher because it allowed me to see things from a different perspective. Pain can bring about positive change as we move along our individual life journeys. Sometimes the experience of feeling pain isn't pretty, but we have an opportunity to grow because of it.

Understanding and feeling love is heightened when we understand and feel pain, even though in times of pain we can lose the connection between who we are, and God. I believe it's the yin and yang principle. We know black is black because we can measure it against white. Cold is cold because we have felt heat, and so on.

It's easy to doubt that our Higher Power, or our spirit guides, or the Universe are present to assist us as we learn our lessons along the path we've chosen. Be not afraid, however; simply ask and it shall be given to you. For further information on this subject I suggest the book, *Ask and It Is Given*, by Jerry and Esther Hicks.

It took years for me to reach the point where I could "observe myself observing myself." This may sound like a really strange thing to say, but I could, after much practice, actually observe myself doing and saying things.

Why is that important? Here's an example: After much practice, I developed the ability to understand how I reacted to people, more exactly, the way I judged others. In the past I could, without thinking about it, make a rash judgment about someone based on what I could see.

Now, however, whenever I come in contact with other people, I observe myself getting ready to judge them based on what I see, and I can stop myself and say, "Hank, you don't have all the information about that person, so let those judgments go."

My friend, Bill, once said, "Hank, try to meet people on a soul level. Look into their eyes and search for their soul. That's who you communicate with. Then you're not just seeing a body standing in front of you. You can see their magnificence." I've discovered it's freeing to be able to do that now.

I've committed to causing peace and harmony in my daily existence. To achieve this, I must desire those things to the point that I am willing to heighten my sense of well-being. Stated another way, I make the conscious choice to raise my level of spiritual vibration.

It isn't so difficult to do once you've decided to be calm and peaceful, and that you want to live a life filled with serenity. There was a time when I kept bringing chaos into my life because I kept complaining about how chaotic my life was. To my way of thinking now, all that did was to reinforce the "bad vibes" as I kept making it my reality by thinking about those things so much.

If you think about making your reality one filled with peace and harmony, eventually that is exactly what you will have in your life. It really does work that way.

Chapter Sixteen

Full Circle

*"We need to take good care of our bodies. We need to have
a positive mental attitude about ourselves and about life. And we need to
have a strong spiritual connection. When these three things are balanced,
we rejoice in living."*
—Louise L. Hay, from *Heal Your Body*

T his, the final chapter, outlines several thoughts regarding the *power of grief*, and the effect it has on people who experience the loss of a loved one, whether it's a child or an adult.

I believe that loss is an opportunity to deepen and grow spiritually as a direct result of that loss. The death of my son, Dan, gave me the opportunity to explore a deeper meaning for my own life. I have also thought deeply about Dan's life and his life's purpose for the short time he was here. That exploration transcends my grief now and profoundly involves the relationship I have with God and my own mortality. The time I spent analyzing my life sparked my desire to change my life which, to this day, continues to be a work in progress.

* * *

One of the miracles Dan left with me was the opportunity to seek answers to questions that are in fact unanswerable. Questions like: "Why did Dan have to leave us so early in his life?" "Why did it have to happen to our family?" "What might we have done differently to save Dan?" "Was his death my fault, and did I do something wrong in my life that caused his death?" "Was God punishing me or my family?"

Those are questions that I wrestled with early in my grieving process. However, as the years have passed, I have come to a completely different comprehension of Dan's death. There are many other questions that I asked, but suffice it to say the journey through it has been enlightening. I've grown immensely in my spirituality because of that experience.

*   *   *

Through the years, as I explored the meaning of Dan's life, I constantly tried to reconcile his purpose in life with the level of my grief. Now I know that was a way to ease the pain of losing him.

Exploring who I thought I was gave me insight into who I wanted to be, and it fashioned the idea of changing how I thought about life and death. Perhaps that transformational realization was inevitable for no other reason than self-preservation.

Taking a closer look at who I was also dovetailed with looking at my family background, which involved my understanding that both positive and negative family dynamics existed. I originally thought that Dan's passing was my problem alone. The pain and anger I felt led to my aberrant behavior which blocked out the feelings of the rest of my family. I've come to realize that the grieving experience was much more complex and it involved many other people in addition to me.

Memory flashback: There was a time, several weeks after my son passed over, that I remember waking up around four in the morning. I got out of bed and shuffled to the kitchen to stand at the double sliding doors facing the large backyard. I stood there awaiting a sign, hopeful I would see him in one form or another. After ten minutes or so, I went back to bed and slept. I was exhausted.

When I awoke sometime around seven in the morning, my eyes clicked open and I had that fleeting moment when I realized who I was and what had happened. I simply didn't want to be me and I remained in bed, paralyzed, unable and unwilling to get up. But eventually those dark days of grief slowly evolved into something that resembled a new "normalcy."

I share this experience with you because it's a vivid reminder of how severe grief can dominate our lives. It will, if we let it, dominate our thinking for years to come. Unchecked, it will rob us of a peaceful life. Forgiveness is the beginning of healing.

Surviving deep emotional grief is difficult at best, and a change regarding the perspective of grief is vital.

For me, it was necessary if I was to survive. At first, I was paralyzed by it. Years later, the grieving process became an opportunity and catalyst for real personal change and growth.

The miracle that I live now allows me to see joy for Dan because I believe he has passed "back home" into the spirit world. This isn't a cop-out by any stretch. My level of spirituality has deepened and changed with an understanding of who we both are.

It's a cliché, I know, but the question of "are we an earthbound person having an occasional spiritual experience, or are we spiritual beings having an earthly experience" rings true. I believe we fit into the second part of that statement.

In our American society, religious beliefs play a role in the grieving process as well. I reconciled my relationship with my Higher Power, and while it took many years to accomplish it, I'm now back on speaking terms with God.

*   *   *

I met my friend Judith, a holistic counselor, one afternoon to discuss the power of grief and the grieving process. We both agreed that the experience of losing a child ranks right up there as one of life's most horrific experiences.

As time has passed, however, and in my case it's now more than twenty-five years since Dan made his transition into the spirit world, the sting has lessened a great deal. Yet the pain of not having him physically in my life remains vividly hurtful and I suspect the feeling will never change. In a seemingly strange way, now I am okay with his passing because I have reconciled his death as an experience that was clearly his destiny and not mine, even though the experience changed my life.

As Judith and I were talking, an analogy relating to my son's experience flashed in my mind: I was standing next to a building that had just exploded for no apparent reason, as far as I could tell. I felt the heat. I felt and experienced the pain of getting burned; but the reality of it was that I didn't have anything to do with the building exploding in the first place. I was witness to it and I was stunned, confused, hurt, and even angry as I wondered what had actually happened.

For me, at this stage in my grieving process, that is basically the same scenario as losing someone dear to you. I had no control over the experience or of what caused the loss. The bottom line is, and in my case at least, I had to live through the experience and deal with it. Like it or not, it was my reality.

In dealing with the experience I found it helpful to try to gain some understanding relative to what we know about the destiny of those who leave us. In essence, if you believe half of what is written about destiny, whether it's your own or someone else's, you begin to pull yourself away from the tragedy and start to think about what the karmic manifestation of the person's passing really means.

For instance, I've noticed that when I attend a wake or a funeral of a person who is very old, many of us say, "Oh well, he or she had a long life." We act as though it's okay that they died, no questions asked, their time was up. However, go to a funeral of a younger person and everyone stands around mulling over what happened and what actually caused this tragedy. We question the meaning of the young person's untimely death. Was it this young person's destiny to leave this earthly existence so soon?

The exploration of one's life's purpose suddenly comes into question and we ponder the relevance of one's life-span versus fulfilling one's life's purpose . . . or are they interrelated?

This probably sounds like a strange statement, but I'm not so sure there is an answer to why someone leaves this earthly incarnation when they do. Oh, sure we can mutter, "It was God's will," but tell that to someone who recently lost a loved one and then let's talk about the look of rage you saw on their face.

Guess what? I suspect there is no answer. We simply do not have that information available to us at this point.

*   *   *

No doubt about it, the entire process of grieving is complex. I believe in the idea that there are phases or steps in the grieving process, as Dr. Elisabeth Kübler-Ross suggests from her research. She points out that our emotions can flip back and forth from one phase to another. In my case, that's exactly what took place, and that speaks to how difficult it is to move through the grieving process in a seamless manner.

It wasn't easy for me and at times it sure wasn't pretty. The emotions involved were many and varied. One minute I seemed to have reconciled with myself regarding, "Why did this happen?," and then the emotions had swung all the way over to flat outrage that it *did* happen. In retrospect, the anger I felt dragged on for a longer period of time than I would have chosen, but I simply could not believe and accept what had happened to me and our family, let alone what happened to my son.

I learned many things in the process, but first and foremost was how strong my ego is. In the years I let my ego drive the grieving process, it put me in a position that caused more harm than good. With my focus being on what I needed as opposed to looking at what was truly Dan's destiny, I lived in fear and let anger dominate my thoughts and actions.

If at all possible, I'd recommend that a grieving person ought not to embrace that line of thinking and behavior for an extended period of time. Seek out good counsel and get professional help.

I realize that everyone deals with grief in their own way. Some people never get over the trauma of losing someone dear to them. Still others make it to the acceptance phase rather quickly. As I reflect on my experience, the drive to find an answer and the need to have a sense of peace about it came through a heightened awareness of my spirituality.

I don't consider myself religious in the strict sense of attending church each Sunday under the penalty of a serious sin, as I was taught when I was younger. Those days are gone forever. My daily meditations continue to open up a whole new way for me to stay in touch with my Higher Power/God.

In a moving and powerful article written by David Roberts, "The Miracle of Stating Your Intent During Your Grieving Journey," he states this about his daughter's death: "Today, I have made a conscious decision to become more spiritually aware while embracing a path of enlightenment that is uniquely my own. The lessons that I continue to learn continually change the storyline of my journey. Change has resulted in continued spiritual growth that has kept me alive amidst the challenges presented by Jeannine's death. We all must find and embrace our own unique paths to enlightenment and spiritual fulfillment."

My grieving process has allowed me to deepen spiritually, and that has made a difference for me relative to trying to understand the meaning of losing a child. I've read a ton of material on the subject of grieving, but in the final analysis it's my faith in God that has carried the day. In fact, more correctly, it carries each day.

*   *   *

Through the years, I've had conversations with many people who have lost someone dear to them. Almost everyone mentioned, in some fashion, that they remembered something personal about their loved ones that they now recognize as a sign.

It takes on profound meaning, especially when a certain song is heard or when they see a "sign" they believe clearly shows that their loved one is nearby or close to them. I experienced that at Dan's funeral. As I recounted earlier, we stood in mournful silence and watched a monarch butterfly land on top of the casket and sit there. For the many years that have followed, whenever I see a monarch butterfly flutter on by, I say a silent prayer to Dan and acknowledge "his presence."

The rock star Elton John has a hit song titled "Daniel." To say the least, several of the lyrics are emotional for me, such as these words: "Daniel, my brother, your eyes have died, you see more than I ..." That entire song haunted me for years. At this stage or phase in the grieving process, however, I am able to smile and simply acknowledge the song, or the butterfly, and say a prayer. No longer do I need to get emotionally wrapped up with the signs, although I am quick to add that I don't discount them as silly.

I suppose a part of this realization is that those of us who grieve don't want to stop grieving for fear that the memory of our loved one will be lost. Nobody wants to let go of the memory of a loved one.

*   *   *

In the early years of grieving, probably for some five to six years after Dan's passing, I had a need to tell everyone I talked to what had happened to my family. I believed they needed to know I was a dad who had lost a son.

As time went by, however, I began to realize that many other people experienced trauma and yet they were living normal lives. Eventually, my need to share my experience and my need for sympathy no longer dominated my life.

The need for sympathy was certainly an integral part of my grieving process. It also contributed to my excessive use of alcohol. How many times have you heard some stressed person say, "Gee, I need a drink to help me relax," or "I need a drink to take the edge off"?

The same was true when I felt sorry for myself. Interestingly enough, however, it wasn't until I stopped drinking that my need for sympathy began to subside. In the early years of grieving I never "connected the dots," so to speak, that the more I drank alcohol, the more it exacerbated my need to feel sorry for myself.

Surround yourself with friends who will listen to you, offer advice to assist as you grieve, and who will be there when you start falling into the morass of painful memories. This support is very important if we are to find our way to being healthy and whole.

*   *   *

The fallout from grief has many faces: depression, anger, disbelief, the feeling of abandonment and deep sorrow, even the question of whether it's possible to ever live a normal life again. It takes hard work and time. But life goes on, doesn't it?

For many years, the thought of never being able to speak to my son again was almost overwhelming. My friends were instrumental in helping me with that. Even though it dominated my thoughts, I often told my friends the loss was beyond sad because the separation from my son was permanent, forever.

It was like placing a long-distance telephone call and no one picks up on the other end—ever. The fantasy was that I knew the line was working because I placed the call, but there was never a response. Nothing. Nada. El zippo. And the really sad part to deal with was the fact that there would *never* be a response.

If you are serious about getting healthy, it is worth my repeating the importance of surrounding yourself with loving, caring friends. I was fortunate to have several male friends who stayed with me when I needed to blow off steam. The ranting and raving worked wonders, and to this day I still—though I admit it isn't often—vent my frustrations out loud.

Years ago, as I ran mile after mile training for a marathon or a triathlon, both my friends John and Andy put up with a lot of my uncontrollable babbling. Running around several of the lakes in Minnesota each day was more than cathartic for me; it was essential.

The learning curve regarding grief and the grieving process has come full circle. I respect grief and the power it can have over our minds and lives. I will not say I totally understand it, but I have a pretty good idea as to how to react with it in my life. I'm not afraid of it and I embrace the idea that feeling and experiencing grief is healthy. Grieving, especially for those of us who have lost a child, is a lifetime event. It will never go away or bring them back. What is crucial to our well-being is our ability to deal with it in a healthy way. That will always remain constant.

My hope for you, who have made it this far in this book, is that you may be filled with a sense of love and that you will find peace in your life. I know for a fact that my son, Dan, is with me. I know it because I have made the conscious choice to keep his memory alive and so he remains close to my heart.

* * *

As I mentioned previously, with the exploration of the meaning of grief in my life, many thoughts and ideas have come to light. There are four excellent books that I found to be incredibly powerful, helpful, and comforting in understanding how we are connected to the spirit world.

The first is: *Growing Up in Heaven: The Eternal Connection Between Parent and Child*, by James Van Praagh.

The second is: *Dying to Be Me: My Journey from Cancer, to Near Death, to True Healing*, by Anita Moorjani.

The third is: *Joseph: Simple and Profound*, channeled by Susan Burns and written and compiled by Judith Struck.

The fourth is: *Proof of Heaven: A Neurosurgeon's Journey into the Afterlife*, by Eben Alexander, M.D.

The following is an excerpt from the third book mentioned above. *Joseph: Simple and Profound* is a discussion that took place between Susan Burns, the channel for Joseph, and Judith Struck, her friend and collaborator. I believe the Joseph Collective explains the meaning of the grieving process thoroughly and to the point, on a spiritual level. Grief is not to be feared, but to be embraced, as bitter as it may be in the beginning.

Grief as a Growth Process: From the Joseph Collective:

Joseph says: Grief is the conscious acknowledgment that something that you have treasured greatly and is of importance to your existence and well-being has been taken away. Its thought and emotion has stopped being in your existence. You do not yet know how to reconstruct your existence.

Question: *Can grief start before the death or loss has occurred?*

Joseph: Of course, it is the process of reconstructing one's existence.

Question: *Once existence is reconstructed, is grief over?*

Joseph: Once the grief is utilized in any way that is of value in the existence, it is over. This is beautiful. There comes a time when you are exposed to the knowledge that reconstruction of your existence is your free will. Do you wish to use the grief and have it become your fate? Or do you wish to become an embodiment of the experience, instead of the experience becoming an act of awakening. You have no limitations on what you wish to do with your existence. Once you have knowledge and trust, you love yourself and The Creator. And you have that moment when you can put grief aside and look at it lovingly as the fuel that kept you going so that you did not end your own existence.

Question: *Grief is an opportunity for growth then.*

Joseph: It makes you look at everything. It is also protection. You hang on to grief while you are healing.

The physical manifestation of grief is a huge experience. Without grief many would end their experience of living. Your grief kept you safe. Do you understand that?

Question: *I thought my responsibility to my child kept me alive, not my grief.*

Joseph: Being wrapped in a shroud of grief allows a person to maintain his existence while moving ahead little by little. It is the grief that is walked with, that becomes most intimate. All should love their grief. There are times when all will grieve. Do not fear it; embrace it.

Epilogue

Vibrations

I have two dear friends. Steve, who since I have known him, has been a great teacher in all matters of developing spirituality. And Judith, the counselor and holistic healer who keeps me thinking about healthy choices and how to stay on a spiritual path.

We meet one day a week and talk endlessly about being stronger, more committed followers of a path that will bring us peace, harmony, and hopefully, enlightenment. We have spent many hours discussing books similar to the four that are mentioned in the previous chapter. Both Steve and Judith also have an uncanny ability to *increase their vibration* to a high spiritual level. They are very holy people. It's a marvel and a blessing for me to be with them.

I, like them, strive to work each day so that I consciously attempt to heighten my vibration to a new level of awareness of who I am. But it wasn't always that easy for me to grasp exactly what heightening my vibration really meant. It sounded so esoteric at first that I couldn't get the drift of how to make it real in my life.

Judith suggested I reread what Joseph had to say about it in the book, *Simple and Profound*. He states it as this: "Once you understand that every action is free will, the next thing you will immediately understand is that when you take an action you have to know whether you are taking it in love, fear, anger, joy or any other emotion. When you are aware that you are using free will with love and joy you will know that you are close to the Creator at that moment." I think that is the answer, plain and simple, and yes, profoundly stated.

However, prior to my getting to that level of awareness, I had to do considerable work to find out who was the "me" inside of me! So, the whole notion of being able to heighten my vibration started with getting in touch with what I was "bringing to the dance," so to speak. Completing the work to discover who I really am was difficult and at times it caused me to question why I was even thinking about these things in the first place. Like, why bother? I thought I was in pretty good shape psychologically and spiritually at that point in my life. Talking things through with Steve and Judith was marvelously enriching, as new ideas from so many different sources came to light. New information emerged and the art of self-knowing that was presented allowed me to "step through the door" to a new awareness.

To me now, heightening my vibration means to live consciously with the daily presence that involves sharing my gifts with others. Being in service to others is another way to increase my vibration, and as Joseph said, if it is done with the freedom of choice, you walk a little closer to the Creator. How marvelous that is!

So, increasing my vibration doesn't have a "feel" to it. It's not like you're getting a "vibe" or a slow, warm feeling. You do have the sense that you are in a place that feels right. Your soul rejoices and sends you a peaceful, easy feeling. Being aware of my attempt to heighten my vibration also allows me to make choices throughout the day that bring both happiness and peace into my life. For those of us who have spent so many years not knowing what happiness and peace feel like, it is profound to finally arrive at that place of knowing. Heightening my vibration brings me to a different level of existence. Marvelous, isn't it?

Working at a level where I stay "awake" each day has brought me inner peace. Good-bye to turmoil; welcome, joy and happiness. Lest you think I'm preaching that I'm in La La Land all day long, I'm not. But even on the days when things are a challenge, I can still look at situations as "opportunities" to discover a new way to solve something that looks or feels difficult.

I like to believe that all of this has brought inner wisdom, but who knows about that? I surely don't and I certainly don't pretend to be wise. All I know is that what I've experienced has "opened my eyes" to the inner me and I am so very thankful for the lessons I have learned.

Thank you, Daniel. I owe you one.

Love,
Dad

Daniel at ten years of age with a friend.

Daniel as a Cub Scout at twelve years of age.

The Maly Boys haming it up . . . Timothy, on the right, Daniel (second from the right, at fifteen years of age), and Matthew and Michael.

Hank Maly with the "boys" today: Matt, Hank, Tim, and Michael.

A monarch butterfly. Just prior to Dan's casket being lowered, a monarch perched on top of the casket. It remains a meaningful symbol.

Appendix

The Twelve Steps of Alcoholics Anonymous

1. We admitted we were powerless over alcohol—that our lives had become unmanageable.
2. Came to believe that a Power greater than ourselves could restore us to sanity.
3. Made a decision to turn our will and our lives over to the care of God as we understood Him.
4. Made a searching and fearless moral inventory of ourselves.
5. Admitted to God, to ourselves, and to another human being the exact nature of our wrongs.
6. Were entirely ready to have God remove all these defects of character.
7. Humbly asked Him to remove our shortcomings.
8. Made a list of all persons we had harmed, and became willing to make amends to them all.
9. Made direct amends to such people wherever possible, except when to do so would injure them or others.
10. Continued to take personal inventory and when we were wrong promptly admitted it.
11. Sought through prayer and meditation to improve our conscious contact with God, as we understood Him, praying only for knowledge of His will for us and the power to carry that out.

12. Having had a spiritual awakening as the result of these Steps, we tried to carry this message to alcoholics, and to practice these principles in all our affairs.

Bibliography

Alcoholics Anonymous Worldwide Services Inc. *Alcoholics Anonymous—The Big Book*. New York: 1976.

Alcoholics Anonymous Worldwide Services Inc. *The Twelve Traditions of A.A.* New York: The A.A. Grapevine Inc., 1952.

Alexander, Eben, M.D. *Proof of Heaven: A Neurosurgeon's Journey into the Afterlife*, New York City: Simon and Schuster Paperbacks, 2012.

Bach, Richard. *Illusions: The Adventures of a Reluctant Messiah*. New York, NY.: Delacorte Press, 1977.

Ellis, Albert, Ph.D., and Robert A. Harper, Ph.D. *A Guide to Rational Living*. Chatsworth, CA: Wilshire Book Co. Paperback, 1975.

Fields, Rick, with Peggy Taylor, Rex Weyler, and Rick Ingrasci. *Chop Wood, Carry Water: A Guide to Finding Spiritual Fulfillment in Everyday Life*, New York, NY: Jeremy P. Tarcher/Putnam, Penguin Putnam, 1984.

Foundation for Inner Peace. *A Course in Miracles*. Farmingdale, New York: Coleman Graphics, 1975.

Frankl, Viktor. *Man's Search for Meaning*. Boston: Beacon Press, 1959.

Gladwell, Malcolm. *The Outliers: The Story of Success*. New York, NY: Little, Brown and Company, The Hachette Group, 2008.

Gray, John. *How to Get What You Want and Want What You Have*. New York, NY: Mars Productions Inc., HarperCollins Publishers, 1999.

Hay, Louise L. *You Can Heal Your Life*. Carlsbad, CA: Hay House Publishers, 1984.

Hicks, Esther and Jerry. *Ask and It Shall Be Given*. Carlsbad, CA: Hay House Publishers, 2010.

Lao Tzu. *Tao Te Ching #64*. New York: Barnes & Noble Classics, 2005.

Moorjani, Anita. *Dying to Be Me: My Journey from Cancer, to Near Death, to True Healing.* Carlsbad, CA: Hay House Publishers, 2010.

Piper, John, the Desiring God organization, 2601 E. Franklin Ave., Minneapolis, MN 55406. 2012.

Roland, Paul. *How to Meditate.* Distributed in the USA by Publishers Group West, Ulysses Press, 2000.

Sanford, John A. *Healing and Wholeness.* New York: Paulist Press, 1977.

Shapiro, Ed, and Deb Shapiro. *Be the Change: How Meditation Can Transform You and the World.* New York, NY: Sterling Publishing Co., 2011.

Sharma, Robin. *The Monk Who Sold His Ferrari.* New York: HarperCollins, 1997.

Struck, Judith, and Susan Burns. *The Joseph Collective: Simple and Profound.* Jacksonville, FL, 2012.

Tolle, Eckhart. *The Power of Now.* Vancouver, BC, Canada: Namaste Press, 1999.

Van Praagh, James. *Growing Up in Heaven: The Eternal Connection Between Parent and Child.* New York: HarperOne Publisher, 2011.

Zukav, Gary. *The Seat of the Soul.* New York: Simon and Schuster, 1989.

Songs:

"I Am Woman," Helen Reddy

"You Can't Always Get What You Want," The Rolling Stones

"The Impossible Dream," Robert Goulet

"I Can See Clearly Now," Johnny Nash

About the Author

H enry R. "Hank" Maly was born and raised in New York City. His professional career spans more than thirty-five years in the field of nonprofit fund development. He is a former university administrator, and his fund development expertise includes: annual funds, planned giving programs, principal gifts, and capital campaigns. He has also designed public relations and marketing strategies in support of fund-raising programs. He served as vice president and chief administrator of development programs at Saint Mary's University (MN), Western Wisconsin Technical College (WI), the Bermuda Biological Station for Research (BD), Manhattan College (NY), and Sacred Heart University (CT). He has supervised, mentored, and directed professional staff in designing plans of operation, establishing budgeting guidelines, and "best practice" procedures.

During his career, Hank has provided counsel to over one hundred fifty national not-for-profit institutions. Prior to establishing his own executive search firm in 2000, he was vice president at Ast/Bryant Consultants in Executive Search in Stamford, CT.

He currently leads executive-level searches with institutions in healthcare, higher education, and social service agencies at Maly Executive Search, in Ponte Vedra Beach, FL. He is a former professional baseball player with the Cincinnati and Minnesota Twins organizations.

Hank and his wife, Dr. Maggie Cabral-Maly, live in Florida and have five grown children and six grandchildren.

www.ingramcontent.com/pod-product-compliance
Lightning Source LLC
Chambersburg PA
CBHW020432290526
45785CB00002B/813